SUMMA
OF
THE OQUAL CYCLE

THE 84-YEAR RHYTHM OF HUMAN CIVILIZATION

FIRST EDITION | 2023

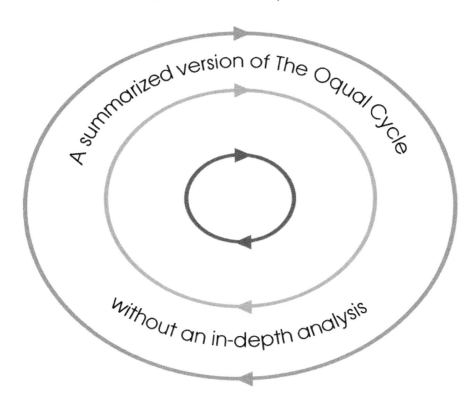

A summarized version of The Oqual Cycle

without an in-depth analysis

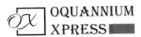

OQUANNIUM
XPRESS

AMJAD FAROOQ

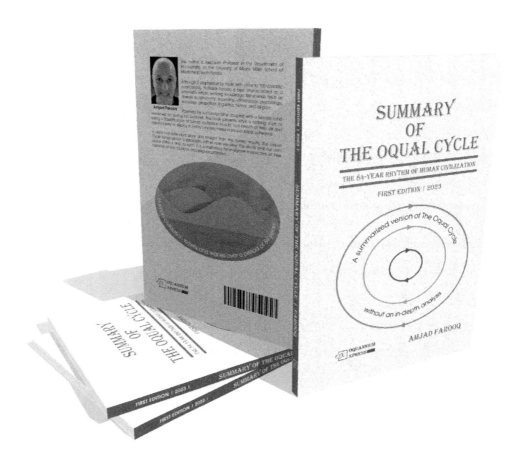

SUMMARY
OF
THE OQUAL CYCLE

THE 84-YEAR RHYTHM OF HUMAN CIVILIZATION

FIRST EDITION | 2023

www.oqualcycle.com

Book Essentials
Final Version on 2023-07-28
First Published on 2023-05-05
Published by Oquannium Xpress
Dimensions: 6"W x 9"H x 1/4"D
Length: 98 pages (32 kilowords)
Approximate Reading Time: 6 hours

Book Formats
ISBN 978-1-960887-09-2 | Ebook (EPUB)
ISBN 978-1-960887-10-8 | Digitalbook (PDF)
ISBN 978-1-960887-11-5 | Audiobook (MP3)
ISBN 978-1-960887-12-2 | Paperback (B&W)

Book Page
www.oqualcycle.com

OQUANNIUM XPRESS
Miami • Florida • USA
www.oquannium.com

CONTENTS

| 1 | PREFACE

Today, almost every nation-on-earth is teetering on the brink of a societal meltdown as it finds itself in the midst of a sociopolitical upheaval, the like of which has not hitherto been witnessed in our lifetime.

Yet, hardly anyone realizes that like a winter that returns every year, such a concerted turmoil across the globe is also periodic due to what I have dubbed the "oqual cycle"—with the adjective "oqual" coined from Latin and literally meaning "84-year" with the oqual cycle therefore essentially being the "84-year cycle".

Admittedly, most public institutions around the world not only seem to have lost credibility but they have also seemingly become irrelevant.

Such a once-in-a-lifetime synchronization of dire sociopolitical straits across much of the globe is no coincidence but rather written in the stars thanks to the mysterious spell of oqual cycle on human civilization.

Not only here at home in America but friends and frenemies from every corner of the world also confide in me:

> "What happened to our civil liberties that we once had taken for granted during much of our earlier lives?"

> "What happened to what were once our rock-solid institutions that provided stability and direction in the face of adversity?"

> "What happened to the good old institution of marriage and our moral compass that once defined who we were?"

> "What happened to the rather upbeat zeitgeist of our earlier lives?"

Well, they have all been temporarily oqualled (or silenced) rather than being forever quelled due to the dire spell of oqual cycle that began a quarter-of-a-century ago almost at the outset of 21st century.

However, the good old days are just round the corner and inching ever closer so as to herald the beginning of a new dawn of hope and prosperity after the dust from the looming World War III has settled in about a decade or so as the oqual cycle draws to a close.

What in the world is oqual cycle?

On the basis of scientific reasoning and mathematical modeling of history over the past 600 years, the oqual cycle posits that human civilization seemingly undergoes a sweeping global reset once every 84 years on average in order to purge itself of a plethora of wrongdoings from the societal ills through excesses and imbalances to transgressions amassed over that multidecadal period.

Unfortunately, there is no free music as one must pay the piper.

Indeed, such a societal reboot (or revitalization) is typically accomplished through a global conflict with the potential to not only wreak havoc but also strike fear into the hearts and minds of people on an apocalyptic scale so that they can put their sociopolitical differences aside and come together for the common good of the world at large.

The oqual cycle therefore lends human society a subtle albeit deadly mechanism to break ties with its dysfunctional past in order to begin anew rather than being held hostage from moving forward under its own weight, or even worse, continue down the rabbit hole in perpetuity with the potential for self-destruction.

More specifically, the oqual cycle posits that the sociopolitical progress of human civilization does not follow a linear course but rather it waxes and wanes in a cyclical manner over a period of 84 years due to what appears to be its coupling with the orbiting of the second outermost planet Uranus around the Sun.

Put another way, the overall human progress waxes and wanes in a sinusoidal manner over the course of oqual cycle in a similar fashion to the waxing and waning of the Moon over the course of a lunar month.

In fact, almost every facet of human civilization from politics through economy to climate appears to be beholden to an 84-year rhythm that propagates in sync with the oqual cycle in a manner reminiscent of our daily and annual rituals.

The oqual cycle is thus essentially a lower-order harmonic of the daily and annual cycles in that the trio seemingly act in a concerted fashion to orchestrate the full gamut of our extraordinary and complex lives.

Of particular note is the salient observation that Uranus appears to exert a subtle control over human civilization by virtue of its ability to modulate the terrestrial climate in a sinusoidal fashion in sync with the oqual cycle in a manner akin to the annual climate cycle dictated by the orbiting of Earth around the Sun.

Admittedly, the unprecedented rise in global temperature witnessed over the past quarter-of-a-century is in no small part due to the Uranian spell on our planet and, as such, global warming is expected to not only plateau out but also head south as the current oqual cycle draws to a close over the next decade or so.

Likewise, the wrath of natural disasters from droughts through flooding to storms with an increasing frequency and intensity seen over the past quarter-of-a-century also seems to be largely due to the cyclical flux of our planet undergoing a self-cleansing process under the watchful eye of oqual cycle rather than a direct consequence of human activities.

While the drummed-up specter of global warming seems to be nothing more than a hyperbole hatched by devious actors around the globe in order to advance their propaganda, there appears to be nevertheless a seemingly upward trend in global temperature over the long run though far from being anywhere near as apocalyptic as that forecast by climate scientists.

Importantly, the oqual cycle not only serves as a model par excellence for making sense of the rapid climate change swamping our planet but also the ongoing sociopolitical trials-and-tribulations of our own times that in no small part elicit a wistful yearning for the rather sweet memories of our recent past from the second half of the 20th century.

To say that the oqual cycle represents a Rosetta stone of human civilization that should help us navigate our future with rational wisdom in lieu of blissful ignorance would be to put it mildly.

Taken together, The Oqual Cycle is a must-read for everyone in that it not only transcends national, ethnic, political, religious, and demographic boundaries but it will also become your most-trusted companion to guide you as you navigate uncharted landscape of your life—the younger you are, the more relevant the oqual cycle is to your life.

|2| PROLOGUE

In 1971, I took my first breath in a nondescript abode planted in the middle of nowhere and shrouded in utter wilderness in rural Mirpur—a city located in the foothills of Himalayas in the northeastern region of Azad Kashmir in Pakistan.

Since my early childhood, I have been awestruck by stories of uncannily-similar upheavals paying us homage time and again.

My beloved grandmother often used to share anecdotal accounts of her forefathers and their belief that every century was like a revolving year with many shared features but on an extended timescale.

While attending university in England during the 1990s, I would become familiar with the oft-repeated cliché: "History repeats itself!"

After moving to America as a postdoctoral scholar a couple of years before the 21st century rolled in, I would learn that while history does not repeat, it nevertheless rhymes and chimes as if it were an integral part of our DNA.

More recently, I would learn that the rise and fall of great powers typically occurs over a cyclical pattern of roughly between 80-120 years as theorized by the Polish-American political scientist George Modelski in his 1987 book titled "Long Cycles in World Politics" [1]—though Modelski's model is based on some questionable data and misinterpretation of historical facts, not to mention that the author is obsessed with the notion of each new century ushering in the rise of a new hegemonic power at odds with reality and, in doing so, he completely dehegemonizes the towering roles that the likes of Spain and France played in shaping the world during much of the 16th and 18th centuries, respectively.

Next, I would stumble upon the work of American historians William Strauss and Neil Howe published in their 1997 book titled "The Fourth Turning" [2]—although difficult to read particularly with regard to its biblical approach rather than a scientific one, I was nevertheless able to curate the central premise of Strauss-Howe model that can be summed up as human civilization cycling through a long human life that spans a period of between 80-100 years with each cycle ending in a crisis of epic proportions.

	Oqual Cycle	Annual Cycle	Daily Cycle
Periodicity	84 years	1 year	24 hours
Quarterly Equivalent	21 years	3 months	6 hours
Monthly Equivalent	7 years	1 month	2 hours
Seasonal Equivalents	Spring, Summer, Autumn, and Winter	Spring, Summer, Autumn, and Winter	Morning, Afternoon, Evening, and Night
Celestial Origin	Orbiting of Uranus around the Sun	Orbiting of Earth around the Sun	Spinning of Earth on its polar axis
Functional Significance	Global reset	Annual rituals	Daily activities

Comparison of oqual cycle with the daily and annual cycles

▶ For further details, see The Oqual Cycle

However, according to the mathematically-driven work of Russian-American ecologist-turned-anthropologist Peter Turchin published in his 2016 book titled "Ages of Discord" [3], such cycles of human civilization are envisioned to last between 150-200 years—though Turchin's model is based on historical records that barely stretch back three centuries and it is therefore not clear how the author can make such outlandish claims against the backdrop of a rather limited timespan of data at his fingertips.

Tellingly, the aforementioned books paint a very confusing picture that leaves one wandering whether the cycles of human civilization last 80, 100, 120, 150, or 200 years—or, perhaps, they occur randomly without a fixed periodicity in which case the whole thing becomes somewhat murky stripping a logical mind of any real enthusiasm of paying heed to such doctrine.

Being a logically-driven mind to the quartic power coupled with an analytical and perfectionist approach to life thanks to my Virgoan cosmotype, I was understandably dumbstruck by the lack of a methodical strategy adopted by the authors in the aforementioned triad of models proposed for the cyclical nature of human civilization.

Admittedly, genuine cycles such as our daily and annual rhythms operate over a predefined timespan, and cycles without a fixed periodicity represent nothing more than a conjecture rather than a serious scientific framework.

That line of reasoning coupled with a nagging curiosity would lead me to launch my own investigation to look into what is arguably the single most important aspect of understanding our society, and through this highly-rewarding process, I was finally able to connect the dots between time and space as I developed the theory of oqual cycle using mathematical modeling and scientific reasoning to account for the cyclical nature of human civilization in a succinct and logical manner on the basis of tons of historical data both at qualitative and quantitative level.

In order to fully comprehend the recurring spell of oqual cycle on our lives, this book therefore delves deep into the causes that bring about eerily-similar revolutions in human civilization every 84 years on average.

Nevertheless, the book provides a logical rather than an exhaustive treatment of history and how it continues to shape human civilization with particular emphasis on connecting the dots between archetypal (or quintessential) events and trends that seem to repeat at remarkably regular intervals of 84 years on average.

In other words, the major historical events represent constituent elements of a larger multi-tier 84-year cascade rather than isolated cases.

Unlike the rise and decline of human civilizations over the course of millennia as documented by the works of European scholars such as Oswald Spengler [4] and Arnold Toynbee [5], the oqual cycle directly impacts our own lives due to the fact that its periodicity equates to an average human lifespan.

Needless to say, the oqual cycle bears huge implications for us at an individual level and how we view the world at large.

In a manner that our understanding of the cyclical nature of a day or a year helps us plan our lives accordingly, the oqual cycle likewise unpacks our own successes and failures in life in that they very much happen to be an intricate function of the ups and downs in our society over which we have little or no control.

Why certain generations for example consistently view the world through rose-colored glasses while others are flabbergasted at their naivete also becomes crystal clear due to the differential spell of oqual cycle on our lives—it matters a lot not only where we are born but also when we are born.

In light of the ongoing sociopolitical bedlam across the globe showing no signs of easing, The Oqual Cycle bears the potential to become our best companion in its ability to guide us through our worst insecurities yet lend a comfort with the promise of a new dawn of optimism and prosperity in the not-too-distant-future.

The Oqual Cycle is indeed indispensable for the sociopolitical health of nations.

It should serve as a reminder to the-powers-that-be to avoid falling into economic quagmires such as debt trap and money printing at the wrong time lest they take the whole nation down with them into a deep canyon between a rock and a hard place with self-destruction all but guaranteed.

	Timespan	Annus mirabilis	Annus turnilis	Annus horribilis	Hegemon	Hegemonic Wars
OC1	1451-1534	1451	1493	1524	Portugal	Fifth phase of Italian Wars (1521-1530)
OC2	1535-1618	1535	1577	1608	Spain	Sixth phase of Eighty Years War (1599-1609)
OC3	1619-1702	1619	1661	1692	Netherlands	Glorious Revolution (1688-1689) Nine Years War (1688-1697)
OC4	1703-1786	1703	1745	1776	France	Russo-Turkish War (1768-1774) US Independence War (1775-1783) Anglo-French War (1778-1783)
OC5	1787-1870	1787	1829	1860	Britain	Crimean War (1853-1856) Indian Mutiny (1857) American Civil War (1861-1865) Franco-Mexican War (1861-1867)
OC6	1871-1954	1871	1913	1944	Britain	World War II (1939-1945) Chinese Civil War (1945-1949) Indian Partition (1947) Arab-Israeli War (1948-1949)
OC7	1955-2038	1955	1997	2028	America	Russia-Ukraine War (2022-date) World War III (circa 2028)
OC8	2039-2122	2039	2081	2112	China	World War IV (circa 2112)

A systematic calendar indicating the unfolding of each oqual cycle (OC) since the birth of Modern Age in 1451

▶ For further details, see The Oqual Cycle

Should great powers pay heed to The Oqual Cycle, the quasi-apocalyptic wars that have hitherto paid us homage at least once in a lifetime could altogether be averted.

The Oqual Cycle is also a godsend for the well-being of our planet in that it identifies the disruptive forces that must be kept at bay lest their cooperative action leaves our world on the precipice of a mental collapse.

A once-in-a-millennium book, The Oqual Cycle will not only lead to a paradigm shift in our perception of human civilization but it is also a must-read for an intellectual and curious mind craving for an answer to what in the world is going on, why it is going on, and when they can expect to see the back of hard times that somehow appear to have become endemic to our society since the outset of 21st century.

On a personal note, I wish I had been cognizant of such a phenomenal aspect of our society from an early age so that I had been well-prepared in advance of the trials-and-tribulations of my prime years rather than making sense of them now in a retrospective manner.

In all, the book is divided into six chapters.

The first chapter serves as a primer for understanding the essential principles of oqual cycle.

Once this prerequisite has been met, the readers are fully equipped to browse other chapters in any sequence they so wish in order to gain an in-depth understanding of oqual cycle with respect to key facets of human civilization such as politics, culture, xenophobia, economy, and climate.

All told, the book walks the reader through the current sociopolitical upheavals unfolding across the globe and what potentially lies on the other side of the bedlam after all the nuclear dust has settled and humanity once again begins to rise from the ashes over the next decade or so courtesy of the mysterious spell of Uranus on our planet.

What has Uranus got to do with all this?

CONCURRENCE BETWEEN URANIAN SOLSTICES AND GLOBAL RESETS

Once every 84 years, Uranus enters its southern winter solstice—the southern midwinter point when the southern pole of Uranus is minimally exposed to direct sunlight over the course of its one full turn around the Sun.

In line with what humanity has endured over the past five centuries, the year during which such a solstice occurs appears to be the annus horribilis due to the fact that it typically coincides with the oqual cycle reaching its crescendo and unleashing the worst of its destructive rage upon our civilization.

Since the birth of Modern Age in 1451, the annus horribilis of oqual cycle has befallen humanity in 1524, 1608, 1692, 1776, 1860, and 1944.

Spaced apart by exactly 84 years, those were really-really horrible times that amounted to nothing short of a hell-on-earth and the like of which is encountered only once-in-a-lifetime.

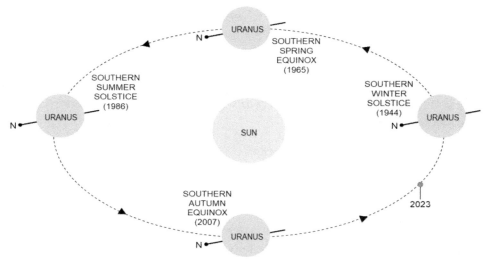

With the last one occurring in 1944, Uranus is poised to enter its next southern winter solstice in 2028

▶ For further details, see The Oqual Cycle

Not only was each annus horribilis noted above flanked by a synchronized-and-synergized wave of deadly conflicts unfolding across the globe but also bore witness to civil wars breaking out across many nations and culminating with the establishment of a nouveau sociopolitical system under a new world order.

For example, 1944 was sandwiched between the destructive World War II (1939-1945) coupled with the dreadful Holocaust (1941-1945) on one side, and the bloody Indian Partition (1947) along with the chaotic births of the State of Israel (1948) and People's Republic of China (1949) on the other—America would emerge as the new hegemon taking up the reins from Britain.

Likewise, 1860 was flanked by the deadly Crimean War (1853-1856) between Russia and Turkiye coupled with the Indian Mutiny (1857) against the British colonialists on one side, and the American Civil War (1861-1865) along with the Franco-Mexican War (1861-1867) on the other—Britain would hold onto its global dominance though closely checked by the rapid rise of America just as the 19th century bid farewell.

On the same token, 1776 was preceded by the Russo-Turkish War (1768-1774) and followed by the American Independence War (1775-1783) coupled with the Anglo-French War (1778-1783)—America would become a sovereign nation and Britain emerged as the new hegemon taking up the baton from France.

Prior to that, 1692 was straddled with the deadly Nine Years War (1688-1697) between France and Netherlands with the latter supported by various European powers including England due to its own existential crisis of the Glorious Revolution (1688-1689)—France would emerge as the new hegemon taking up the mantle from Netherlands.

Before that, 1608 was marred by the consequential sixth phase of the Eighty Years War (1599-1609) between Spain and Netherlands with each supported by various European powers—Netherlands would emerge as the new hegemon taking the helm from Spain.

Finally, 1524 was underscored by the 1529 Treaty of Cambrai in the midst of the fifth phase of the so-called Italian Wars (1521-1530) pitting Spain against France for the control of Italian peninsula as well as global dominance with each side supported by various European powers—Spain would emerge as the new hegemon and Portugal having passed on the torch.

Why should I care about our checkered past?

OUR SOCIOPOLITICAL TITANIC HAS ALREADY HIT THE ICEBERG WITH OUR LEADERS SCRAMBLING TO AVERT THE UTTER CARNAGE WAITING AHEAD

Once every 84 years on average, human society reaches a nadir when it becomes boxed-cornered-and-trapped under its own weight of a plethora of wrongdoings from the societal ills through excesses and imbalances to transgressions amassed over the course of oqual cycle.

This self-inflicted trauma is further exacerbated by Mother Nature which seemingly reserves the worst of its scourge on humanity by virtue of its ability to unleash a barrage of natural disasters just when we are at our worst and least prepared.

Such synergism between Mother Nature and humanity's unraveling plunge the society into an even deeper sociopolitical crisis.

Today, that is exactly the status quo around much of the globe as sociopolitical quandary of virtually every nation has turned into an insoluble Rubik's cube.

Not only that but many nations even believe that they are being battered by Mother Nature for their excesses and imbalances though they understand not that such retribution is nothing more than a stroll in the park compared to what awaits them ahead over the next decade or so.

Arguably, our sociopolitical system has been hitting a new low with each passing year with no signs of troughing out since the outset of 21st century.

	The Oqual Cycle [This Book]	Ages of Discord [3]	The Fourth Turning [2]	Long Cycles in World Politics [1]
First Published	2023	2016	1997	1987
Historical Window	1400-2023	1700-2016	1500-1997	1500-1987
Quantitative Data	Yes	Yes	No	No
Periodicity	84 years	150-200 years	80-100 years	80-120 years
Periodicity Fixed	Yes	No	No	No
Systematic Calendar	Yes	No	No	No
Previous Cycle	1871-1954	1780-1919	1866-1945	1900-??
Current Cycle	1955-2038	1920-??	1946-??	??
Next Cycle	2039-2122	??	??	??
Geographical Region	Global	United States	United States	Global
Global Synchronization	Yes	No	No	No
Celestial Orchestrator	Uranus	None	None	None
Societal Domains	Universal	Sociopolitical History	Sociopolitical History	Sociopolitical History
Author Name	Amjad Farooq	Peter Turchin	William Strauss and Neil Howe	George Modelski
Author Background	Biophysicist and Polymath	Ecologist and Anthropologist	Historian (WS) Historian (NH)	Political Scientist
Author Nationality	Pakistani-British-American	Russian-American	American (WS) American (NH)	Polish-American
Author Lifespan	1971-date	1957-date	1947-2007 (WS) 1951-date (NH)	1926-2014

Comparison between The Oqual Cycle and previous models proposed to account for the cyclical nature of human civilization

▶ For further details, see The Oqual Cycle

In metaphorical terms, our sociopolitical Titanic hit the iceberg nearly a quarter-of-a-century ago and since then it has only continued to sink with no sign of lifeboats anywhere in plain sight.

Ironically, every sociopolitical step taken by our leaders to fix the leak has only served to exacerbate the plight of our sinking Titanic due to the fact that such a Band-Aid has always been a slippery slope.

Instead of sending out an SOS call to the masses to come forward and make sacrifices during what have been rather difficult times over the past quarter-of-a-century, the-powers-that-be have been going out of their towers to make life even easier for hoi polloi in an attempt to remain politically popular rather than what was best for their nation.

For example, over the past couple of decades, the global financial system has been flooded with decatrillions-of-dollars of printed money coupled with virtually every nation taking on ever more debt to purportedly address the dire economic straits of the masses.

Yet, such generous handouts have been akin to an addict being given a license to continue to overdose on heroin in that they only served to fuel the reckless lifestyle of hoi polloi having become accustomed to living beyond their means and becoming an ever-rising burden on society.

Just as the addict encounters their rendezvous with destiny once-in-a-lifetime, so does humanity as a whole so as to purge and cleanse our society of its reckless violations of the laws of nature in lieu of continuing down the rabbit hole in perpetuity with the potential for self-destruction.

Such a proofreading mechanism, which can also be viewed as a reality check or quality control, revitalizes human civilization by enabling it to break ties with its dysfunctional past so as to begin anew just as the oqual cycle moves past its annus horribilis.

When is the next annus horribilis due?

THE NEXT ANNUS HORRIBILIS IS LURKING ON THE HORIZON

While the oqual cycle is not set in stone, it nevertheless begins and ends with each full turn of Uranus around the Sun once every 84 years—a timespan dubbed "oquannium" that is to oqual cycle what annum is to an annual cycle.

In particular, the oqual cycle can be viewed as a tale of two diametrically-antagonistic halves: a constructive phase of relative peace followed by a destructive spell of sociopolitical upheaval, with each lasting some 42 years.

Having nominally begun in 1955 and set to bid farewell in 2038, the current oqual cycle is in the latter stages of its destructive spell with the year 2028 in line to become the next annus horribilis—the year during which Uranus is poised to enter its next southern winter solstice.

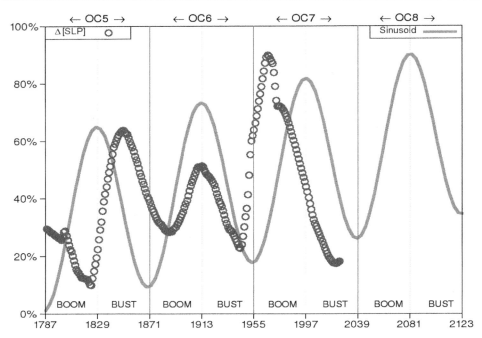

Human population growth waxes and wanes in sync with the progression of oqual cycle such that baby boom is followed by baby bust and vice versa

► For further details, see The Oqual Cycle

If 2028 is the annus horribilis of the current oqual cycle, then 2039 will be the annus mirabilis of the next one in a manner similar to 1955, 1871, 1787, 1703, 1619, 1535, and 1451 since the outset of Modern Age.

While annus horribilis is indicative of the fact that the worst of the fallout from our wrongdoings amassed over the course of oqual cycle is already upon us or approaching its crescendo, annus mirabilis all but guarantees the beginning of good times if they have not already arrived on our shores years earlier than anticipated.

Taken together, the ongoing sociopolitical crisis will soon morph into a global conflict of epic proportions that will end no earlier than annus horribilis (2028) of the current oquannium (1955-2038) but by no later than annus mirabilis (2039) of the next cycle (2039-2122) so as to acquiesce to a new dawn of hope and prosperity—such a forecast is deduced with a high degree of confidence in line with the recurring spell of oqual cycle on our civilization.

As the saying goes, no pain no gain.

Indeed, a large-scale global conflict with the potential to not only wreak havoc on an astronomical scale but also strike fear into the hearts and minds of people appears to be a prerequisite for breaking ties with our past and old traditions so as to revitalize human society and usher in a brighter tomorrow under a new world order spearheaded by a nation that has proved itself as the manufacturing powerhouse head-and-shoulders above its competitors.

Without such a real-life horror show a la hell-on-earth, people on opposite sides of the sociopolitical spectrum refuse to see eye-to-eye in order to come to a consensus necessary to rid the society of its wrongdoings amassed over the course of oqual cycle.

In particular, when a society has gone astray and lost its moral compass as is the case across much of the globe today, havoc combined with fear appear to be blessings-in-disguise in that they serve to jumpstart a new beginning so as to reset our sociopolitical system.

On the one hand, fear appears to be an incredibly-effective therapy for deranged individuals to come to their senses and exercise humility after having lost the moral compass or having become accustomed to living beyond their means and a burden on society over the course of oqual cycle.

On the other hand, havoc seems to facilitate the removal of old traditions so as to usher in new technologies coupled with creating megatons of highly-rewarding jobs that motivate otherwise discouraged individuals to get back to work just as the human society sets about rebuilding from scratch.

As for the loss of human life on a humongous scale, it seems that biology is also in on the act collaborating closely with the oqual cycle to pull off its own magic of pitting humanity against a deadly audit so as to proofread its own product before continuing further afield and, in doing so, ensuring the survival of the fittest at the expense of the weak.

No matter how advanced and progressive our civilization may come to be viewed as, it seems that humanity simply cannot shake off the oversight of biology and the wrath of nature.

While it pains me a great deal to deliver such a dire forecast of what lies ahead in the near future, I am only a messenger who is reverberating echoes from the past that seem to be repetitive and unavoidable at remarkably regular intervals of 84 years on average.

Still, a new dawn of good-old-shiny-happy days is on the horizon and will likely arrive some time during the 2030s in a manner akin to the beginning of relatively prosperous times during the 1950s, 1870s, and 1790s savored on American soil and across much of the globe.

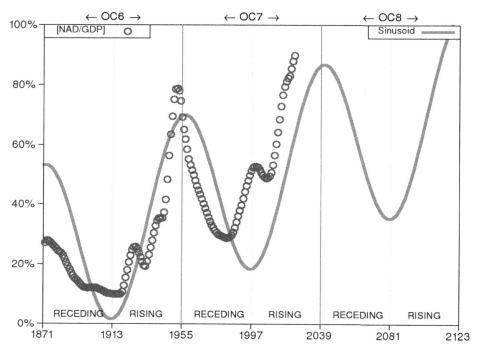

A nation's debt burden ebbs and flows in tandem with the progression of oqual cycle producing a perpetual tale of two contrasting halves underscored by a receding tide followed by a rising tide and vice versa

> ▶ For further details, see The Oqual Cycle

However, the ongoing sociopolitical upheaval will get multiples worse over the next decade or so before we see the light at the end of the oqual tunnel.

In other words, the human society not only finds itself in a bind but has also been rolling downhill since the outset of 21st century and it will continue to do so for at least another decade before it reverses course and begins to climb uphill once again with a renewed vigor just as it did some 84 years ago during the 1950s.

In particular, the decade centered on annus horribilis (2028) of the current oquannium (1955-2038) does not bear good omens as it will not only be paralyzed by deadly conflicts and civil wars unfolding across the globe but the odds of a nuclear war breaking out over that period are also statistically high.

With that ominous decade roughly stretching from 2023-2033 having just kicked off, we can already see the tip of the nuclear iceberg threatening to capsize our civilization like never before.

While the countdown has already begun, many are quick to dismiss the utter bedlam waiting ahead as nothing more than fear-mongering on the pretense that none of such doom and gloom has ever borne fruition in their lives except that it only occurs once-in-a-lifetime.

Admittedly, hardly any adult who faced the scourge of World War II (1939-1945) is alive today nor any adult today will be alive some 84 years from now when annus horribilis (2112) of the next oquannium (2039-2122) rolls in.

What is however indisputable is the fact that when one makes a deal with the devil, they cannot expect to have an angel waiting for them on the other side.

Why is a nuclear war all but a mathematical certainty?

TRILLIONS WERE NOT INVESTED IN NUKES JUST SO THAT THEY WOULD BE FOR THE SHOWROOM

As the oqual cycle draws to a close, with the current one poised to do so in 2038, the battle for determining the new world order gets under way across the globe so as to usher in a new dawn under a nouveau sociopolitical system.

Not only does such a global conflict straddling the annus horribilis outshine its predecessor due to the emergence of ever more destructive killing machines over the course of oqual cycle but the world leaders also do not shy away from using the most lethal arsenal at their disposal as they lock horns to settle the contest for the control of the world and its resources.

Since the dawn of the current oquannium (1955-2038), global powers have hitherto funneled trillions-of-dollars toward developing a paraphernalia of nukes in order to gain a military edge over their rivals.

To believe that such apocalyptic weapons are only for the showroom would be to sweep history under the rug.

Paradoxically, that ought to be a huge credit to humanity for being so resourceful in that it does not invest in something it will never use.

Still, when the specter of a nuclear war is contemplated, it is often viewed as nothing more than a razzmatazz better suited for science fiction than becoming a real-life documentary.

Yet, the same audience would put the probability of a nuclear war befalling humanity at 10% in any given year—little they realize that such odds amount to a mathematical certainty of a nuclear war breaking out over the next decade.

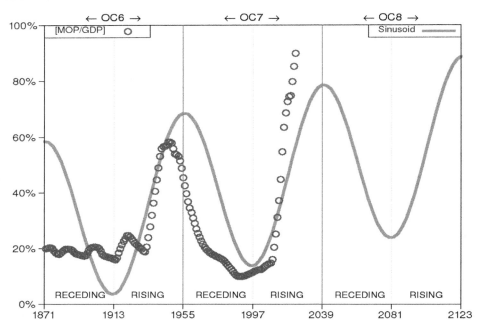

Money printing by central banks ebbs and flows in tandem with the progression of oqual cycle producing a perpetual tale of two contrasting halves underscored by a receding tide followed by a rising tide and vice versa

▶ For further details, see The Oqual Cycle

Importantly, the hope that the most destructive weapon at one's disposal will not be unleashed is nothing more than a folly that has come back to haunt humanity time and again.

Nevertheless, the looming nuclear war will in all likelihood be a tactical one with the potential to turn a few cities into ghost towns rather than an all-out apocalypse for humans have a built-in evolutionary mechanism to exercise restraint and tamp down collateral damage when faced with utter annihilation.

The notion that humanity could one day nuke itself into extinction is nothing more than a hyperbole.

Still, the looming threat of a societal collapse is not lost on those with means—while they are yet to learn about the dire spell of oqual cycle on human civilization, many uber-wealthy individuals have already begun to shop for either giant bunkers or citizenships in far-flung safe-havens in preparation for all hell breaking loose on earth over the next decade or so.

Although such wealthy fools and their entourage of financial advisors are drawing parallels between today and the zeitgeist of 1980s, we are in fact currently traveling through a similar time and space as we did some 84 years ago vis-à-vis our sociopolitical system in line with the oqual theory supported by a barrage of eye-popping data rather than opinion.

Thus, the next decade or so will be very much akin to the 1940s in a manner reminiscent of recurring annual seasons.

Just as the annual winter does not necessarily have to replicate its predecessor, the same also holds true for the oqual cycle as it draws to a close.

While the looming global conflict is unavoidable, it is hard to conclude if it will be a shadow of World War II (1939-1945) or whether it will make its predecessor look like a dress rehearsal.

Still, given the 800-pound gorilla of our wrongdoings amassed over the past several decades, it is hard to imagine anything other than the latter outcome for the magnitude and intensity of the global conflict befalling humanity at the dusk of oqual cycle appear to be proportional to the extent of our deviations from the laws of nature as evidenced through the unfolding of one crisis after another with each plunging us ever deeper into a canyon without a rescue over the past quarter-of-a-century.

Will the ongoing Russia-Ukraine War turn into a full-fledged World War III?

NATO HAS ALREADY STARTED FIGHTING RUSSIA THROUGH A PROXY WAR

While the seeds for the ongoing dire sociopolitical straits were planted nearly quarter-of-a-century ago by America and its European lapdogs via a double whammy of first through the expansion of NATO and then closely dogged by the decades-long self-destructive 9/11 Wars, they have finally begun to sprout around the globe with a vengeance.

In 2022, after decades of provocation by NATO, Russia's full-fledged invasion of Ukraine came hot on the toes of the 84th anniversary of Poland's annexation by Nazi Germany as the previous oquannium (1871-1954) neared its end.

In 1939, few at the time believed that such a preemptive action by the Nazis against Poland was the beginning of a global conflict as World War II (1939-1945) came home more than two years later with the Japanese attack on Pearl Harbor in 1941 and, in doing so, drawing the then rising global power of United States into the war.

Unsurprisingly, the echoes of 1939 have once again begun to reverberate with the 2022 Ukraine-Russia conflict showing no signs of abating.

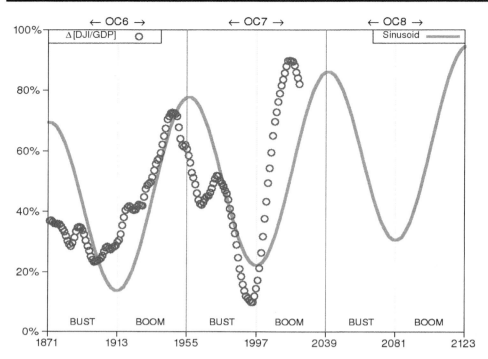

Returns in the stock market ebb and flow in tandem with the progression of oqual cycle producing a stock bust followed by stock boom and vice versa

▶ For further details, see The Oqual Cycle

Just as Nazi Germany and Soviet Union signed a pact to divide Poland between them in 1939, so did Russia and China some 84 years later in 2022 to go about their territorial business with a mutual understanding and cooperation in their attempt to reclaim what they believe to be their destiny in Ukraine and Taiwan, respectively.

With a 20/20 hindsight in a decade from now, the ongoing Ukraine-Russia conflict will come to be viewed as the start of World War III though it is yet to come home just like its predecessor some 84 years earlier.

In fact, more than a year into the conflict, the 2022 Ukraine-Russia tussle has not only gained enormous inertia but it has already turned into a NATO-Russia war in that without the overpowering military support from the West, the Siberian Tiger would have long toppled its much smaller Western neighbor.

To add salt to Russian wounds, NATO has refused to engage in diplomacy as it ups the ante in order to escalate the conflict already threatening to spiral out of control.

Bluntly put, NATO has already started fighting Russia through a proxy war in what is essentially an unequal contest in that the latter's conventional military power is no match for the West's paraphernalia of hi-tech arsenal and spurs.

Nevertheless, Russia's nuclear capability is something to be reckoned with as the deployment of nukes will not only level the battlefield but also take the NATO bully by the horns without even breaking a sweat.

Sooner or later, the Siberian Tiger will indeed be forced to heavily rely upon its nukes as the NATO-Russia war chugs along in that facing the prospect of a crushing defeat at the hands of its immortal enemy would be simply unfathomable for Russian leaders for whom a world without Russia ought to be no world at all.

It is indeed rare that the opposing sides in a global conflict are equally balanced in terms of their military might.

Accordingly, when one warring party feels frustrated or is facing defeat with conventional firepower as Russia is poised to do so over the next couple of years, it will have no choice but to resort to the deployment of its nukes as a last resort to salvage something out of nothing.

In what I call "Oquandra", the power of oqual cycle to forecast sociopolitical future is personified as the modern-day equivalent of Cassandra.

> "Only fools would call Russia's nuclear saber-rattling a bluff", Oquandra says.

> "Russia can no longer get out of the mess it has trapped itself into without the use of nukes", Oquandra adds.

> "The Siberian Tiger with a barrage of nukes at its disposal will soon begin to feel like a Cornered Tiger and you know what happens next", Oquandra goes onto lament as she breaks the rather bad omens.

Admittedly, given its gigantic landmass and sparsely-populated cities unlike many Western nations with densely-crowded metropolises, Russia would clearly enjoy a strategic advantage when a nuclear war does finally break out.

In a nutshell, the probability of World War III becoming a nuclear one is all but unity.

Nukes not playing even a tactical role in such a looming conflict flanking 2028 would be at odds with a time-tested human tradition, particularly when they are already on the bench warming up to be introduced at a short notice in the deadly game of thrones that is all but upon us.

To argue against such a highly probable outcome would be like saying that one can go through the whole winter without a snowstorm.

That is possible but not a realistic outcome.

How does America benefit from the outbreak of World War III?

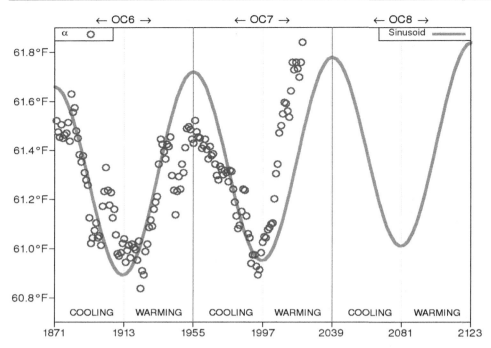

The global temperature ebbs and flows in lockstep with the progression of oqual
cycle producing a perpetual tale of two contrasting halves underscored by a
cooling period followed by a warming spell and vice versa

► For further details, see The Oqual Cycle

WORLD WAR III LENDS AN UNCOMFORTABLE SOLUTION TO AMERICA'S SOCIOPOLITICAL UPHEAVAL

World War III would be a boon for America in that it will provide a perfect smokescreen (or camouflage) for a barrage of nation's Ponzis from social security through national debt to dollar hegemony teetering on the precipice of going up in smoke any day, not to mention that the looming global conflict will also create tons of opportunities to reboot the nation's old-and-degenerate economic engine from scratch just as World War II did some 84 years earlier.

Not only will World War III put an end to decades-long economic stagnation in America and across much of the globe but it also appears to be the only mechanism to return to those good old days of economic prosperity enjoyed by the masses in line with the oqual theory.

This is due to the fact that the thermodynamic bottleneck holding the socioeconomic system hostage can only be overcome through the release of free energy via a large-scale global conflict.

While those in the upper echelons of global powers understand this thermodynamic rule very well, they are however not quite sure when to get such a transformation underway though their job is made all the more easier given that such timing is largely determined by annus horribilis of oqual cycle.

Toward this goal, America has turned Ukraine into a battleground with monetary and military aid having already exceeded the $100B mark within the first year alone of what is likely to be a long and protracted Russia-Ukraine War undergoing a slow and painful metamorphosis into World War III.

To put that into perspective, Ukraine's economic output runs at $200B annually.

Thus, the $100B windfall for Ukraine would be equivalent to God showering America with a lotto of at least $12T annually—while an unlikely scenario to bear fruition, one cannot imagine how such a godsend could make every American so rich that they could all retire at 18 and never have to work ever again.

Till then, Americans must continue to work if only to pay their bills and fund wars.

Indeed, it is mind-boggling to say the least as to why Americans cannot see the World War III in the making and being bankrolled by their tax dollars.

To add to their incognizance, Western media have already taken victory laps on behalf of Ukraine without even realizing that the Siberian Tiger has not even been awoken yet and what they have so far witnessed is nothing more than a mouse playing with the big cat's tail.

Slumbering it may very well be but Russia is fully aware of the fact that it is fighting America not Ukraine and, when two superpowers lock horns, there can be no peaceful solution.

Rather, utter annihilation of our world is on the cards over the next decade or so as exquisitely forecast by the dire spell of oqual cycle on human civilization.

Has World War III not been debated ad nauseam throughout our lives?

So why should it happen now when it has never happened before?

Had the ongoing Ukraine crisis between two global powers pitting Russia directly against America occurred a couple of decades earlier, it would not in-and-of-itself be a recipe for World War III to break out.

Today, however, the ever-bloating sociopolitical upheaval serves as a catalyst to turn such a crisis into a full-fledged global conflict.

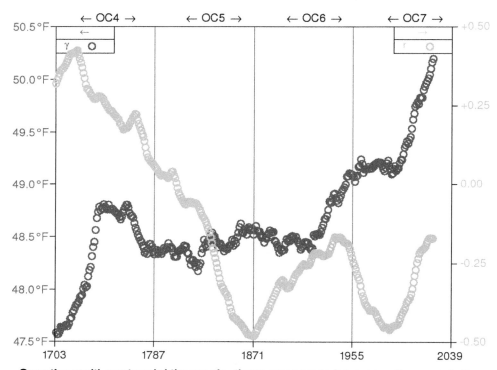

Over the multi-centennial timescale, there appears to be a negative correlation between the global temperature (blue) and the emission of carbon dioxide as probed by the time-resolved Pearson's correlation coefficient (green)

▶ For further details, see The Oqual Cycle

Indeed, the 1962 Cuban Missile Crisis did not lead to a war between the two global powers, much less a global conflict, due to the fact that it transpired against a backdrop of relatively prosperous times that would make the sociopolitical dilemmas of that era look like a stroll in the park compared to what the world is facing today.

Ever wondered why chemists are darn good at solving problems?

Because they have all the solutions!

Not only that but a chemist would also tell you that one can have all the reactants they desire in a test tube but, without a catalyst, they are not going to attack each other nuclearphilically or otherwise.

Today, the sociopolitical upheaval is nothing short of a potent catalyst on the verge of being unleashed to turn the ongoing Ukraine Crisis into World War III.

Add to that the fact that the fools who have been debating World War III since the 1960s are utterly ignorant of history in that the odds of a global conflict dwindle as human society walks past annus horribilis of oqual cycle as it did some 84 years earlier in 1944 but then they begin to swindle as it cycles back to that horrible year as is the case today with the next annus horribilis (2028) barely years away.

With the writing already on the wall without hors d'oeuvres in the hall, one can only disregard the dire spell of oqual cycle at their own peril as it inches ever closer to our day of reckoning.

Given the perpetuity of a plethora of crimes from having normalized a culture of living beyond means through institutional fraud run amok to the hilt to debilitating economic stagnation that continue to bloat by the day, one would be naïve to think that such calamities will somehow disappear and a better tomorrow will emerge by itself.

Heck no!

Such a societal reboot does not occur spontaneously but rather it happens to be an endothermic process.

In a manner that an endothermic reaction requires the input of heat so as to lower the activation energy of the transition state to generate a product, a destructive mechanism with the potential to strike fear and chaos into the hearts and minds of people on an apocalyptic scale seems to be a prerequisite to rid our society of such a baggage of evils so as to make way for a fresh start.

Just as World War II (1939-1945) accomplished that goal some 84 years ago so will World War III over the next decade or so as utter fear and chaos engulf our society and, in doing so, purge humanity of mischief so as to enable it to come to its senses once more.

A brighter tomorrow is indeed on the cards but only after humanity has been handed due retribution for having gone bonkers over the past several decades.

Once a few cities have been nuked into the ground, hardly anyone would indeed be left with the urge to continue a reckless lifestyle of self-indulgence and hedonism nor would anyone dare to put up a Ponzi over the several decades that follow until people's memories of hard times begin to fade away once more.

Unfortunately, such deadly punishment seems to be the only mechanism to put human society back on its track after it has not only lost its moral compass but also moral protractor—one could of course pick them up at WHSmith but why bother learning geometry when bots can do everything for you these days:

> Bot > You: Hey bot!
> Bot > Me: Hello!
> Bot > You: How many angles does the pentagon have?
> Bot > Me: Right now, the Pentagon has only one angle! World War III!

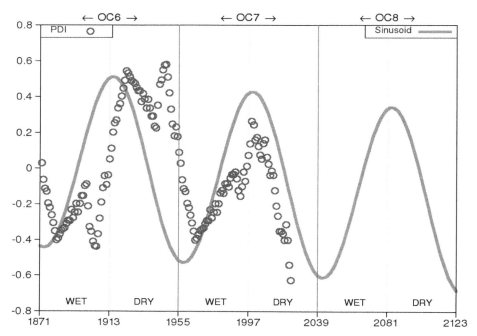

The severity of droughts seemingly ebbs and flows in sync with the progression of oqual cycle producing a relatively wet period followed by a dry spell and vice versa

▶ For further details, see The Oqual Cycle

Admittedly, the Pentagon is gung-ho on turning the Russia-Ukraine War into a global conflict without even realizing the scale of utter carnage waiting ahead.

Can American leaders not see where such escalation could lead to?

After having been on cocaine for decades through running excesses and imbalances at every societal level, America's parable today is akin to an addict who has simply lost control of their life in that every new step that they take in the misguided belief that it will turn their poor state of affairs around only serves to exacerbate their dilemma.

And when everything goes up in smoke at home, they also set the world on fire.

Indeed, the US government is led to believe that a global conflict offers a perfect solution to its sociopolitical upheaval at home and to once again regain global preeminence just as it did some 84 years earlier in the wake of World War II.

After all, what kind of an American capitalist would not want another global conflict where Europe and Asia get razed to the ground and US companies earn trillion-dollar contracts to rebuild them.

That ploy seems quite plausible except that unlike World War II, America will not come out of World War III unscathed as today's world is very different from what it was some 84 years earlier.

With the likes of Russia and China not only vying to hold their own with their hypersonic technology having made the globe look like a small village but, in many ways, the Eurasian nations are militarily far more advanced than the United States would like to believe due to greed and hubris in an echo of Nazi Germany.

And we know how that panned out for Nazi Germany.

Unfortunately, a similar fate awaits America as the time to pass on the baton of global leadership is inching ever closer with the ominous-and-defining decade centered on annus horribilis (2028) of the current oquannium (1955-2038) having already begun.

A contributing factor to America's foxy ploy turning roxy is the fact that the morale within the US Armed Forces (USAF) is at an historic low in an echo of the American society at large.

With United States having bankrupted itself morally and financially through the decades-long 9/11 Wars waged under the guise of freedom and democracy yet driven by the capitalist interests of the wealthy, the rank-and-file of USAF are much more cognizant of America's true intentions today than they have ever been in the nation's 250-year history.

With America's hidden war propaganda having been laid bare, the odds of United States achieving its capitalist goals and goods through World War III therefore do not bode well.

Nor do they bode well for America's whipping boys across the Atlantic.

Unlike some 84 years earlier when they were the belligerents on steroids and precipitated their own self-destruction through World War II, European nations today are completely oblivious to being fooled and tricked into Siberian Tiger's den with dire consequences of being badly mauled and left bruised once again.

It seems that Europe has learned nothing from history.

As the saying goes, those who fail to learn from history are doomed to repeat it.

It is indeed highly probable that Europe will be caught in the deadly crossfire between Eurasia and America for a battle for the control of world's resources as World War III begins-in-earnest over the next couple of years or so.

How will China benefit from the looming World War III?

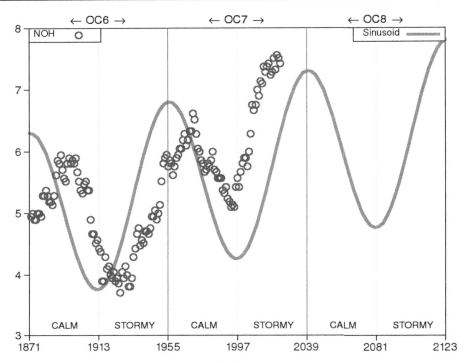

The frequency and severity of storms seemingly ebbs and flows in sync with the progression of oqual cycle producing a relatively calm period followed by a stormy spell and vice versa

▶ For further details, see The Oqual Cycle

CHINA IS RUBBING ITS HANDS WITH SIBERIAN GLEE AND FEET WITH INDIAN GHEE AS IT MANOEUVERS TO TAKE UP THE BATON OF GLOBAL LEADERSHIP

On the other side of the looming conflict, China is aptly and deservedly positioned to emerge as the new hegemon taking up the baton of global leadership from America some time between annus horribilis (2028) of the current oquannium (1955-2038) and annus mirabilis (2039) of the next cycle (2039-2122).

However, such a transfer of global power is unlikely to happen without a showdown between the two superpowers in a manner akin to the fact that the alpha male in a lion pride does not get dethroned by a younger and more hungrier competitor without putting up a fight of his life.

In that sense, the looming World War III can also be viewed as a rite of passage for the newly-minted hegemon to take up the mantle from its predecessor.

But, for China, such a rite of passage goes through Taiwan for without its soul the Asian Giant cannot claim to be whole, much less a leader of the world.

Being fully aware of such a deadly confrontation and coronation waiting on the horizon, China is working round the clock to beef up its military paraphernalia with the Chinese navy today being the largest in the world and rapidly dwarfing its US counterpart—a truly daunting feat that should not be lost on anyone given that the wars are won and lost at sea.

And when it comes to battling it out at sea, preponderance reigns supreme over all else in guaranteeing the triumph as attested by history time and again.

In fact, history shows that the hegemon is often dethroned not because it is no longer powerful enough to knock out its rival but because it lacks the stamina to go the full round due to the low morale within its ranks echoing the rather poor state of the nation as a whole having fallen prey to moral disintegration as a result of self-indulgence and waning zest for life.

When China and America finally square up against each other over the next decade or so, it is quite clear which nation would be fighting tooth-and-nail and which one would be grappling with a low morale—or rather which one of them would be fighting to the death and which one fighting for life.

Top that up with the fact that China has also begun to salivate at the prospect of shepherding the world in accordance with its national interests as it rapidly expands its radius of geopolitical influence around the globe.

That is all the more damning for the Western powers given that the center of economic gravity is set to shift to Asia over the next decade or so after a hiatus of some 500 years.

| 3 | GENESIS

With a knack for logical and quantitative approach to understanding whatever I stumble upon, my curiosity rarely kills the cat.

On the contrary, it occasionally leads me to have a moment of epiphany.

Not only did I recently encounter one such moment of epiphany but also a moment of inertia when I serendipitously came upon the rather ominous but hitherto an undiscovered connective tissue between A and B, where:

- A = The year during which the second outermost planet Uranus enters its southern winter solstice once every 84 years.

- B = The decade centered on that recurring year being accompanied by really-really horrible times to have befallen humanity in that they have hitherto amounted to northing short of a quasi-apocalypse over the past five centuries.

Add to this the finding that tons of centuries-old historical data both at qualitative and quantitative level not only happen to best fit a periodicity of exactly 84 terrestrial years but they also happen to be synchronized with the corresponding Uranian year (which is equivalent to 84 terrestrial years)—while correlation does not necessarily imply causation, it is nevertheless the first step toward developing a theory that appears to be orchestrated by celestial bodies.

Of particular note is the observation that altering such periodicity even by one terrestrial year dramatically throws archetypal events and repetitive patterns into a disarray such that they begin to lack a discernible cyclical trend.

Given that one terrestrial year is to a Uranian year what a 5-day week is roughly to a terrestrial year, one can immediately see how shortening our year to 360 days or lengthening it to 370 days would palpably screw up the cyclicity of our annual rituals within a matter of a decade, if not sooner.

That is exactly what happens to oqual cycle as it goes haywire if one were to alter its periodicity even by one terrestrial year.

So far so good but what exactly is a solstice, you might ask?

Solstice is the timepoint at which the northern (or southern) pole of a planet is minimally or maximally exposed to sunlight during the course of its one full turn around the Sun.

For example, the Earth experiences two such solstices around June 21st and December 21st each year—which respectively mark the summer solstice (the longest day of the year) and the winter solstice (the shortest day of the year) with respect to the northern pole and vice versa relative to the southern pole.

In the context of Uranus, the southern winter solstice denotes the southern midwinter point when the southern pole of Uranus is minimally exposed to direct sunlight over the course of its one full turn around the Sun.

Why do Uranus's solstices mark the midpoint in Uranian winters?

Is such a scenario not at odds with what the Earth experiences?

URANUS EXHIBITS A REMARKABLE IDIOSYNCRASY IN OUR SOLAR SYSTEM

If it were not for our Earth's obliquity (or axial tilt), the sunlight would hit the equator all year round in an equal measure such that there would be no seasonal variations in light or temperature.

One cannot imagine life without seasons on Earth.

However, things are not so rosy on Uranus.

In a manner that the orbital period of Earth around the Sun defines the length of a terrestrial year, the orbital period of Uranus circumscribes one Uranian year—which is equivalent to 84 terrestrial years.

In other words, the Earth completes 84 orbital rotations around the Sun for every round that the Uranus does.

Likewise, the oqual cycle is to a Uranian year what the annual cycle is to a terrestrial year.

And the oquannium is to an oqual cycle what the annum is to an annual cycle.

That is pretty much where similarities between the two planets end and differences begin to emerge when one takes a closer look at the ice giant.

Unlike the rather small axial tilt of 23° for the Earth's polar (or spin) axis with respect to a line perpendicular to its orbital plane around the Sun, the Uranus's polar axis is tilted by a whopping 98° (see Exhibit 3.1).

Thus, unlike the Earth and the other six planets that orbit the Sun with a quasi-upright tilt like a spinning top, Uranus does so practically on its side a la rolling ball (or water wheel) with its spin axis being almost parallel to the orbital plane as if its poles have no qualms about staring directly at the mighty star of our solar system.

Given such an idiosyncratic orientation of Uranus, the Sun continuously shines almost directly on each of its poles during their respective summer solstices—the time point at which each pole reaches its maximal exposure to sunlight during the orbital cycle.

On the other hand, each pole of Uranus is continuously bathed in complete darkness during its winter solstice—the time point at which each pole reaches its minimal exposure to sunlight during the orbital cycle.

Accordingly, such solstices mark the midpoint of a 21-year-long summer (which is essentially one long uninterrupted day without dark) or the midpoint of a 21-year-long winter (which is akin to one long uninterrupted night without light).

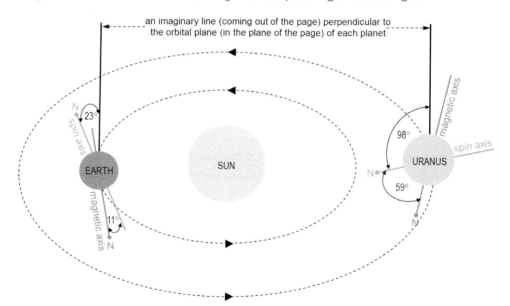

Exhibit 3.1 | Comparison of the axial tilt of Earth and Uranus with respect to a line (solid black) perpendicular to the orbital plane (indicated by elliptical dashed lines) of each planet. The letter N indicates the direction of the north pole of: (1) an imaginary line (solid green) around which each planet spins on its axis; and (2) magnetic axis (solid red) running directly through the center of the magnetic field of each planet. The schematic shown is not to scale.

It is noteworthy that such a framework is in sharp contrast to the Earth's solstices which for their part mark the beginning of a winter or summer due to the rather differential inclination of the Earth's polar axis relative to the Sun—the Earth orbits the Sun with its polar axis being roughly perpendicular to the orbital plane as if its poles are somewhat shy of looking directly at the heart of our solar system.

In addition to its idiosyncratic axial tilt that produces extreme 21-year seasons, Uranus also exhibits many other distinguishing quirks.

While Earth's magnetic field is more or less aligned with its spin axis, it is tilted by a staggering 59° relative to the spin axis of Uranus (vide supra).

Such a lopsided (or off-centered) configuration produces a multipolar rather than a dipolar effect such that Uranus experiences a rather non-uniform magnetic field with its strength being much greater in the northern hemisphere relative to the southern half.

Importantly, a sturdy and uniform magnetic field, as is the case on Earth, is critical to shielding a planet against the constant scourge of solar wind—a moving mass of ionized particles that flies outward at supersonic velocity from the outer surface of the Sun toward other planets including our own.

However, such a shielding against solar wind does not appear to be much of a big deal on Uranus where the poorly-configured setup of magnetic field is further compromised by its flipping on and off like a light switch such that the ice giant gets whipped by the solar wind on a daily basis.

When does Uranus encounter its next southern winter solstice?

On the basis of astronomical data courtesy of Voyager-2 launched by NASA in 1977 to probe the outer space [6], the south pole of Uranus was imaged looking directly and maximally at the Sun in 1986.

In 1986, the ice giant therefore must have been in the midst of its southern summer solstice with the southern hemisphere continuously bathing in sunlight and the northern hemisphere being plunged into darkness (see Exhibit 3.2).

In 2007, 21 years later, Uranus reached its southern autumn equinox when the planet's equator bore the brunt of the Sun's radiation.

In 2028, another 21 years later, Uranus is poised to enter its next southern winter solstice.

Thus, the current oqual cycle is poised to end in 2038 with the next one beginning in 2039—assuming that 2028 marks the midwinter point on the southern pole of Uranus and each Uranian year begins with the start of southern spring from the perspective of earthlings.

How many oqual cycles has humanity encountered since the birth of Modern Age in the 15th century?

Circa 1451, the advent of a fast-moving printing press by the German inventor Johannes Gutenberg revolutionized European civilization in that it allowed mass-production of information that could then be quickly circulated among intellectuals, thereby opening up collaborations and driving technological advances as well as enabling masses to read and write.

Given such a paradigm shift that tilted the balance of philosophical power from Asia to Europe some 500 years ago as Gutenberg's printing press could only print modular letters in lieu of cursive text that formed the bedrock of Asian languages, the year 1451 is used as a reference point to mark the birth of Modern Age.

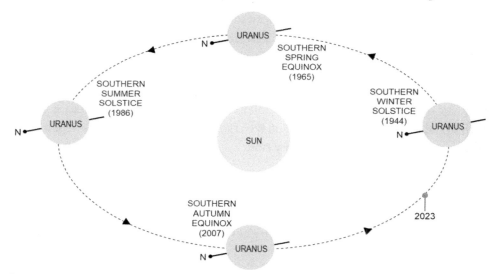

Exhibit 3.2 | A timeline of seasonal changes encountered on the southern hemisphere of Uranus since the last southern winter solstice in 1944. In 2018, the southern hemisphere of Uranus plunged into yet another 21-year dark winter that will last until 2038. Halfway through this winter in 2028, Uranus will encounter its southern winter solstice once again for the first time since 1944 when the southern pole will be minimally exposed to sunlight for the first time in 84 years. The red dot shows the celestial position of Uranus relative to the Sun in 2023 with five years to go until it encounters its next southern winter solstice in 2028. The letter N indicates the direction of the north pole of an imaginary line (solid black) around which Uranus spins on its axis once every 17 hours with the Uranian day being a little more than two-third of its terrestrial counterpart. The schematic shown is not to scale.

Equally remarkable is the fact that the Italian explorers Christopher Columbus and Amerigo Vespucci, who together discovered the New World and laid much of the groundwork for the early maritime technology that enabled humanity to map the world as we know it today, both took their first breath in 1451.

Add to that the fact that the fall of the Byzantine Empire representing the last remaining vestiges of the Roman Empire in 1453, when the Ottomans marched into Constantinople (the modern-day Istanbul), also occurred almost in parallel with the birth of Modern Age (1451-date).

Coincidentally, the year 1451 also happens to be the start of a new Uranian year beginning with the southern spring.

The ice giant must therefore have been onto something as it heralded a new Uranian year with a bang of its own to match so many groundbreaking events unfolding here on Earth in 1451 or thereabout.

Notably, humanity will have experienced seven full bouts (or spells) of oqual cycle between the birth of Modern Age in 1451 and the start of the next cycle in 2039, or arithmetically put: $(2039-1451)/84 = 7$.

With the first oqual cycle (OC1) beginning in 1451 since the birth of Modern Age, the second oqual cycle (OC2) began in 1535 ($1451+84=1535$) with each new one emerging every 84 years thereafter.

The current and seventh oqual cycle nominally began in 1955 and is poised to end in 2038, or arithmetically put: $1450+(7x84) = 2038$.

Importantly, the synchronization of oqual cycle with the Uranian year starting with southern spring and ending with southern winter is corroborated by tons of historical data on human civilization undergoing ebbs and flows over the past five centuries or so.

In particular, a new dawn of sociopolitical order appears to have taken hold on our lonely planet every 84 years on average starting nominally in 1451.

Although it serves as a prerequisite to break ties with our dysfunctional past in order to begin anew, such a global reset is far from being a free lunch but rather occurs only after the piper is paid for our transgressions amassed over the course of oqual cycle.

In line with what humanity has endured over the past five centuries, the year during which Uranus enters its southern winter solstice is what I have dubbed "annus horribilis" in that it typically coincides with the oqual cycle reaching its crescendo and unleashing the worst of its destructive rage upon our civilization.

Since the outset of Modern Age in 1451, the annus horribilis of oqual cycle has befallen humanity in 1524, 1608, 1692, 1776, 1860, and 1944.

Spaced apart by exactly 84 years, those were really-really horrible times that amounted to nothing short of a hell-on-earth and the like of which is encountered only once-in-a-lifetime.

Not only was each annus horribilis noted above flanked by a synchronized-and-synergized wave of deadly conflicts (or hegemonic wars) unfolding across the globe but also bore witness to civil wars breaking out across many nations and culminating with the establishment of a nouveau sociopolitical system under a new world order.

For example, 1944 was sandwiched between the destructive World War II (1939-1945) coupled with the dreadful Holocaust (1941-1945) on one side, and the bloody Indian Partition (1947) along with the chaotic births of the State of Israel (1948) and People's Republic of China (1949) on the other—America would emerge as the new hegemon taking up the reins from Britain.

Likewise, 1860 was flanked by the deadly Crimean War (1853-1856) between Russia and Turkiye coupled with the Indian Mutiny (1857) against the British colonialists on one side, and the American Civil War (1861-1865) along with the Franco-Mexican War (1861-1867) on the other—Britain would hold onto its global dominance though closely checked by the rapid rise of America just as the 19th century bid farewell.

On the same token, 1776 was preceded by the Russo-Turkish War (1768-1774) and followed by the American Independence War (1775-1783) coupled with the Anglo-French War (1778-1783)—America would become a sovereign nation and Britain emerged as the new hegemon taking up the baton from France.

Prior to that, 1692 was straddled with the deadly Nine Years War (1688-1697) between France and Netherlands with the latter supported by various European powers including England due to its own existential crisis of the Glorious Revolution (1688-1689)—France would emerge as the new hegemon taking up the mantle from Netherlands.

Before that, 1608 was marred by the consequential sixth phase of the Eighty Years War (1599-1609) between Spain and Netherlands with each supported by various European powers—Netherlands would emerge as the new hegemon taking the helm from Spain.

Finally, 1524 was underscored by the 1529 Treaty of Cambrai in the midst of the fifth phase of the so-called Italian Wars (1521-1530) pitting Spain against France for the control of Italian peninsula as well as global dominance with each side supported by various European powers—Spain would emerge as the new hegemon and Portugal having passed on the torch.

Other than the quartet of 21-year seasons from spring through summer and autumn to winter, there are also three critical junctures that underscore the oqual cycle as described below:

1) **Annus mirabilis**—The 1st year of oqual cycle that all but guarantees the beginning of good times if they have not already arrived on our shores years earlier than anticipated after the dust from the sociopolitical fallout from the previous cycle has settled. In particular, the decade centered on annus mirabilis marks the beginning of several decades of relative peace and prosperity ahead. For example, good times began across much of the globe around annus mirabilis (1955) of the current oquannium (1955-2038) as fondly remembered through the Golden Age in America (1950-1970), Swinging Sixties in Britain (1960s), and Les Trente Glorieuses in France (1945-1975). Likewise, some 84 years before, annus mirabilis (1871) of the previous oquannium (1871-1954) also heralded decades of relatively happy times as epitomized by the Gilded Age in America (1870-1900), the Late Victorian Era in Britain (1870-1901), and La Belle Époque in France (1870-1914).

2) **Annus turnilis**—The 43rd year of oqual cycle that marks its midpoint (or turning point) when sociopolitical progress of human society begins to turn south and ushers in decades of chaos ahead until they morph into an insoluble maze as the oqual rhythm nears its end. Notably, the turning point is marked by an archetypal crisis during the decade centered upon annus turnilis though none has ever paid heed to such a harbinger of things to come over the decades that followed. For example, the decades-long 9/11 Wars (2001-2021) followed shortly after the arrival of annus turnilis (1997) of the current oquannium (1955-2038). Likewise, some 84 years earlier, World War I (1914-1918) sprang out immediately after annus turnilis (1913) of the previous oquannium (1871-1954). While run-of-the-mill conflicts break out throughout the oqual cycle, large-scale protracted wars such as World War I and the 9/11 Wars not only befall humanity once-in-a-lifetime but they also serve as a primer to plunge the human society into an even greater sociopolitical chaos that ultimately leads to hegemonic wars such as World War II (1939-1945) and the looming World War III as the oqual cycle draws to a close.

3) **Annus horribilis**—The 74th year of oqual cycle during which Uranus enters its southern winter solstice, the midwinter point indicative of the fact that the worst of the sociopolitical fallout from our wrongdoings amassed over the course of oqual cycle is either already upon us or approaching its crescendo. Such a hell-on-earth usually occurs during the decade centered on annus horribilis. For example, annus horribilis (2028) of the current oquannium (1955-2038) is all but set to witness the looming World War III on an epic scale so as to bring about a global reset and usher in a new dawn of hope and prosperity. Likewise, some 84 years before, annus horribilis (1944) of the previous oquannium (1871-1954) was sandwiched between the destructive World War II (1939-1945) coupled with the dreadful Holocaust (1941-1945) on one side, and the bloody Indian Partition (1947) along with the chaotic births of the State of Israel (1948) and People's Republic of China (1949) on the other.

Of particular note here is the fact that the annus horribilis of each oqual cycle is flanked by hegemonic wars—a series of global conflicts that are all but obligatory for breaking ties with our dysfunctional past in order to begin anew under a new world order spearheaded by a nation that has proved itself as the manufacturing powerhouse head-and-shoulders above its competitors (see Exhibit 3.3).

It is also noteworthy that the outbreak of World War I (1914-1918) almost in parallel with the onset of the second half (1913-1954) in lieu of erupting closer to the end of previous oquannium (1871-1954) must not be assumed as being an anomaly.

Rather, World War I marked the archetypal midcycle conflict in a manner similar to the 9/11 Wars that breaks out as the oqual cycle reaches its midpoint and plants the seeds for the decades-long sociopolitical upheaval that is subsequently resolved by an even bigger global conflict.

That it came to be referred to as a world war at all is nothing more than a case of semantics thanks to illogical historians, not to mention that it was renamed from being a Great War to World War I in hindsight in the wake of the outbreak of World War II (1939-1945) a couple of decades later.

From a logical perspective and for the sake of consistency, the honor of the first-ever world war taking place across all corners of the globe in fact belongs to the so-called Nine Years War (1688-1697) fought between the then rising power of France and the decaying empire of Netherlands with the latter closely supported by England and other European nations as the third oquannium (1619-1702) drew to a close with what were once mighty Dutch forced to pass on the baton of global hegemony to Les Gaules.

	Timespan	Annus mirabilis	Annus turnilis	Annus horribilis	Hegemon	Hegemonic Wars
OC1	1451-1534	1451	1493	1524	Portugal	Fifth phase of Italian Wars (1521-1530)
OC2	1535-1618	1535	1577	1608	Spain	Sixth phase of Eighty Years War (1599-1609)
OC3	1619-1702	1619	1661	1692	Netherlands	Glorious Revolution (1688-1689) Nine Years War (1688-1697)
OC4	1703-1786	1703	1745	1776	France	Russo-Turkish War (1768-1774) US Independence War (1775-1783) Anglo-French War (1778-1783)
OC5	1787-1870	1787	1829	1860	Britain	Crimean War (1853-1856) Indian Mutiny (1857) American Civil War (1861-1865) Franco-Mexican War (1861-1867)
OC6	1871-1954	1871	1913	1944	Britain	World War II (1939-1945) Chinese Civil War (1945-1949) Indian Partition (1947) Arab-Israeli War (1948-1949)
OC7	1955-2038	1955	1997	2028	America	Russia-Ukraine War (2022-date) World War III (circa 2028)
OC8	2039-2122	2039	2081	2112	China	World War IV (circa 2112)

Exhibit 3.3 | A systematic calendar indicating the unfolding of each oqual cycle (OC) since the birth of Modern Age in 1451. The first oqual cycle beginning with the Modern Age is denoted OC1 and the ones thereafter OC2, OC3, OC4, and so forth in a chronological order at an interval of every 84 years. Note that the calendar is synchronized with the Uranian year beginning with the southern spring and ending with the southern winter. Hegemonic wars represent a series of global conflicts that break out during the decade centered on annus horribilis of oqual cycle and which are necessary to bring about a global reset so as to break ties with our dysfunctional past in order to begin anew under a nouveau sociopolitical order. Hegemon is the country that emerges as the most powerful nation in the aftermath of hegemonic wars and goes onto set the new world order for at least the next 84 years. To date, Britain remains the only nation to have carried the baton of hegemony for two consecutive rounds of oqual cycle. That is why it has come to be called Great Britain!

It should also be emphasized that while the decade centered on annus horribilis of oqual cycle is typically accompanied by really-really horrible times a la hell-on-earth, humanity is in fact mired in a sociopolitical chaos during much of the second half (over the course of autumn and winter) of oqual cycle in stark contrast to a period of relative harmony enjoyed by the masses during the first half (over the course of spring and summer).

In particular, the fallout from our wrongdoings amassed over the course of oqual cycle reaches a tipping point around annus horribilis in the midst of oqual winter, which for the current oquannium (1955-2038) arrived in 2018 and will last until 2038.

With that in mind, the winter is therefore not coming but it is already upon us.

Needless to say, the next decade or so will be a time of extreme trials and tribulations for humanity-writ-large.

Nevertheless, a new dawn of hope and prosperity awaits us all on the other side of the looming World War III just as the next oqual cycle begins to breathe down our neck with the arrival of 2030s.

How does a planet as far away in outer space as Uranus orchestrate human civilization on Earth?

Do other celestial bodies also have a say in the affairs of earthlings?

THE PHYSICAL BASIS OF URANIAN SPELL ON OUR LIVES REMAINS MYSTERIOUS

Few would doubt the impact of the planet Earth on human civilization from how the daily cycle controls our circadian rhythm to how the annual cycle powers our lives from harvesting crops to breeding.

If the Earth seems so central to our activities, one wonders whether other celestial bodies could also play a similar role in dictating our lives—albeit to a lesser extent as they become more and more distant from our planet.

Indeed, the rotation of the Moon around the Earth dictates the monthly (or lunar) cycle characterized by the ebb-and-flow of ocean tides, migration and breeding of many animals, and even menstruation in humans.

Thus, it would be quite ingenuous to rule out the possibility that the other planets in our solar system somehow modulate terrestrial life (see Exhibit 3.4).

This school of thought is indeed corroborated by a recent study indicating that the gravitational tug (or coupling) between Jupiter and Venus modulates terrestrial climate over hundreds of millennia [7].

In fact, life on Earth would not even be possible without the other planets escorting and providing a convoy of sorts for the jewel in the crown of our solar system.

It should therefore be hardly surprising that being the planetary elephant in our solar system with an orbital period of around 12 years and a magnetosphere that even dwarfs that of the Sun itself, Jupiter likely unleashes its spell on human behavior in a subtle manner.

According to the 2008 book titled "Life Cycles" by the Australian psychologist Neil Killion [8], human beings start a new chapter in their lives every 12 years or so.

In other words, a notable transition occurs in our lives around ages 12, 24, 36, 48, 60, 72, and 84—the latter being the magic number that appears to define the average length of human lifespan.

	Orbital Period / years	Distance (from Earth) / 10^9m	Surface Diameter / 10^6m	Axial Tilt / °	Surface Magnetic Field / μT
Inner Planets:					
Mercury	0.24	92	4.88	0	0.12
Venus	0.62	41	12.10	177.36	0.00
Earth	1.00	0	12.74	23.45	30.60
Mars	1.88	78	6.78	25.19	0.00
Outer Planets:					
Jupiter	11.86	629	139.82	3.13	430.00
Saturn	29.45	1275	116.46	26.73	21.40
Uranus	84.02	2724	50.72	97.77	22.80
Neptune	164.79	4351	49.24	28.32	13.20

Exhibit 3.4 | Key physical properties of the octet of planets in our solar system in the ascending order of their distance from the Sun. Note that Jupiter not only stands out in the crowd for its humongous size but also for its rather gigantic magnetosphere (or the area of space around the planet where its magnetic field has a detectable presence).

In many ways, Killion's theory appears to be very familiar to us.

For example, the onset of puberty in humans occurs around the age of 12.

Around the age of 24, most athletes reach their physical peak while many others get married, become parents, or graduate from university to begin a new phase in their lives.

Around the age of 36, most of us peak mentally and intellectually, and for many academic scientists, they either land their first autonomous appointment as an investigator or their first major grant.

Around the age of 48, many of us are either promoted to the rank of grandparents, managers, or executives, while others begin to see the best of their career achievements in the rearview mirror as they begin to wind down and accept the hard reality that they no longer boast the same energy or enthusiasm that they did a decade earlier.

Around the age of 60, many of us ride off into the sunset wherein we either begin to reap the fruits of our decades-long labor or we face the music for having lived a reckless life.

Around the age of 72, humans usually become fearless as they have nothing to lose careerwise or otherwise, and many begin to speak their mind for the first time ever in their lives—however, in my case, that moment arrived at 12 and has stuck with me ever since even though sailing against the wind would cost me more than an arm and a leg at every stage in my life.

Rest assured, I still have two arms and two legs.

I guess I must have been born with lots of arms and legs. Allahu akbar!

Finally, around the age of 84, most of us bid farewell to Mother Earth.

While Killion's theory is indeed supported by the periodic 12-year transitions in the lives of numerous movers and shakers to have set foot on earth over the past century or so, there are nevertheless going to be many individuals who stand out as an exception to this life pattern though such anomalies should in no way pour cold water over what is arguably an eye-popping model governing our lives.

What impact does Jupiter have on the oqual cycle?

Together with Jupiter and Uranus, Saturn and Neptune make up the quartet of outer planets in our solar system—they are also called Jovian planets for their rather gigantic size due to their predominantly gaseous composition.

The Jovian planets are far from being solitary creatures unaware of each other's footprint in space but rather they are conjoined in a celestial marriage of sorts.

In particular, Uranus appears to be more or less gravitationally coupled with its three neighbors on an 84-year timescale, or a multiple thereof.

For example, with an orbital period of 12 years, Jupiter makes 7 turns around the Sun for every turn of Uranus such that the two planets realign in space with respect to Earth once every 84 years (12x7=84).

Likewise, with an orbital period of 29 years, Saturn would also more or less realign in space with Uranus once every 84 years or so (29x3=87).

With an orbital period of 165 years, the outermost planet Neptune roughly aligns with Uranus once every other Uranian year (165/2=83).

Given that the combined orbital period of Uranus with its Jovian neighbors is roughly 84 years or a multiple thereof, it implies that the three other outer planets are also likely to have a say in governing the oqual cycle.

In particular, such gravitational coupling between the quartet of outer planets likely renders Uranus as an orchestrator of sorts with respect to its ability to modulate terrestrial activities with the trio of Jupiter-Saturn-and-Neptune acting as improvisers, chaperones, or even celestial mirrors to transmit astronomical effects instigated by the ice giant via electromagnetic radiation or gravitational tuning.

It could well be that Uranus is not only in a gravitational tug with its three Jovian neighbors but that their magnetic fields are also coupled such that they act in concert to attune solar wind as it heads toward Earth.

Additionally, the gravitational tug between the Jovian planets could also modulate the axial tilt of Earth such that the total amount of solar irradiance striking our planet oscillates over a period of 84 years.

To be clear, solar irradiance is the total solar energy reaching the Earth via the full gamut of electromagnetic radiation from the high-energy γ-rays and x-rays through ultraviolet-light-and-infrared to microwaves and radiowaves though the latter have negligible impact on heating our planet.

In attuning solar wind and solar irradiance, Uranus along with its Jovian partners could therefore directly modulate terrestrial climate, which may very well be the missing link between the oqual cycle and its celestial origin.

Admittedly, that is exactly what seems to be the case—the terrestrial climate indeed appears to oscillate more or less in sync with the progression of oqual cycle.

Not only that but the Earth appears to alternate between a COOLING period and a WARMING spell, with each stage lasting some 42 years, over the course of oqual cycle.

Strikingly, the COOLING period correlates with a zeitgeist of relative peace and harmony over the first half of oqual cycle whereas the WARMING spell occurs during the second half when our society plunges into decades of utter madness as is the case across much of the globe today.

I should also add that while Uranus may be located in outer space more than a billion miles from Earth, electromagnetic radiation such as x-rays from the ice giant have not only been detected on our planet but they can also reach us faster than a flight from Miami to Gran Manzana.

Thus, the impact of Uranus on our lives is not completely out of the physical realm even though the exact mechanism by which the ice giant orchestrates terrestrial life and climate in sync with its orbital rotation around the Sun unequivocally remains mysterious.

That should hardly be surprising given that our current understanding of the universe is primitive at best and the onus lies squarely on the future generations of astronomers to shed new light on how exactly celestial bodies impact the affairs of earthlings.

Long story short, the lack of a physical basis for the oqual cycle should in no way undermine what otherwise appears to be a Rosetta stone of human civilization.

What exactly is oqual cycle in mathematical terms?

HUMAN PROGRESS PROPAGATES ALONG A HELICAL PATH

In a manner akin to the daily and annual cycles that govern our lives, the oqual cycle dictates the waxing and waning of human civilization albeit over a much longer timespan than its higher-frequency counterparts.

The oqual cycle can therefore be envisioned as being a lower-order harmonic of the daily and annual cycles with which it seems to share many features (see Exhibits 3.5 and 3.6).

For example, the Earth's surface temperature appears to oscillate over a period of 84 years in a manner reminiscent of its dynamics over the course of a day or a year.

On the other hand, the ebbs and flows in our daily and annual rhythms seem to parallel the ups and downs in human civilization over the course of oqual cycle.

Another way to look at the relationship between the oqual rhythm and its higher-order harmonics is through a series of concentric circles with their increasing radii being indicative of the longer period of the corresponding harmonic over which it completes one full oscillation (see Exhibit 3.7).

Admittedly, the central premise of oqual cycle is that the progress of human civilization is akin to a circular ride in a theme park, wherein one gets to see the same view time and again albeit in an uncanny way, rather than propagating along a railway track without any reference to its past.

Needless to say, the oqual cycle puts human progress on the same footing as most natural phenomena wherein things are circling back and forth, or cycling, rather than moving along a linear track.

Think how the darkness-of-the-night follows the light-of-the-day and vice versa in a perpetual daily cycle.

Think how the winter follows the summer and vice versa in a perpetual annual cycle.

Think how the planets orbit the Sun in a cyclical manner, with each completing one full rotation over a fixed period of time.

	Oqual Cycle	Annual Cycle	Daily Cycle
Periodicity	84 years	1 year	24 hours
Quarterly Equivalent	21 years	3 months	6 hours
Monthly Equivalent	7 years	1 month	2 hours
Seasonal Equivalents	Spring, Summer, Autumn, and Winter	Spring, Summer, Autumn, and Winter	Morning, Afternoon, Evening, and Night
Celestial Origin	Orbiting of Uranus around the Sun	Orbiting of Earth around the Sun	Spinning of Earth on its polar axis
Functional Significance	Global reset	Annual rituals	Daily activities

Exhibit 3.5 | Comparison of oqual cycle with its higher-order harmonics.

Add to that a spate of solar cycles driven by the cyclical variation in the number of sunspots on the Sun's surface that modulate terrestrial climate over decadal, centennial, and millennial timespans.

Likewise, as embodied in the so-called Milankovitch Cycles, terrestrial climate is also regulated by cyclical variation in the Earth's movements with respect to its orbital dynamics such as:

1) **Orbital Eccentricity**—The extent to which a planet's orbit around the Sun deviates from a perfect circle. In the case of Earth, such orbital eccentricity varies between a near-circle to a semi-ellipse over a period of roughly 100 kiloyears.

2) **Axial Tilt**—The angle between a line perpendicular to the orbital plane of a planet and its spin axis (also called axial obliquity). Although the current axial tilt of Earth is around 23°, it can fluctuate by at least one degree in either direction over a period of around 41 kiloyears.

3) **Axial Precession**—The wobbling of a planet as it rotates about its spin axis in a manner akin to a top spinning slightly off-center. The Earth takes nearly 26 kiloyears to complete one full axial precession.

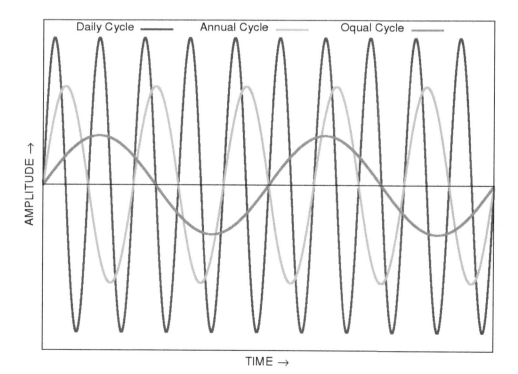

Exhibit 3.6 | Oqual cycle is essentially a lower-order harmonic of the more familiar daily and annual cycles. The simulation shown is not to scale in either dimension.

It is not only our physical world but cyclical phenomena are also a hallmark of biology as one could not imagine life without the likes of:

1) **Kreb's cycle**—Powers virtually all living cells;
2) **Calvin cycle**—Turns atmospheric carbon dioxide into glucose in plants with the aid of solar energy and water; and
3) **Urea cycle**—Transforms the rather toxic ammonia byproduct in our body into urine.

Simply put, cycles are essential to fuel our physical and biological worlds and keep them self-sufficient without the need for an external driver.

In fact, everything in nature is on the move but it is essentially spinning along a circle rather than moving along a line.

That is the reason why our ancestors never found the "edge" of the earth nor we will ever find the "edge" of the universe as neither traces out linearity but rather each curves back onto itself conforming to an infinite circle or a sphere in three-dimensional space.

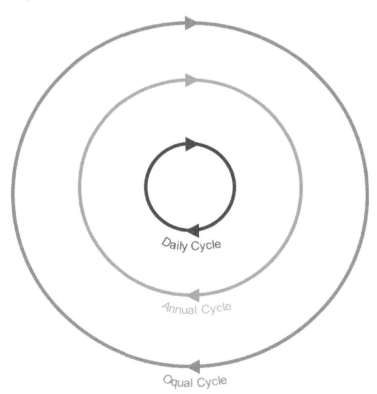

Daily Cycle

Annual Cycle

Oqual Cycle

Exhibit 3.7 | The relationship of oqual cycle to its daily and annual counterparts as viewed through a series of concentric circles with their radii being indicative of the length of the period of the corresponding harmonic. The schematic shown is not to scale.

One therefore does not have to be a rocket scientist to realize that the progress of human civilization must also be circular rather than linear without any relationship to its past.

However, like other natural phenomena, human progress does not merely circle back onto itself—if it did, no progress would be made at all in stark contradiction to our everyday experiences.

Rather, such a spinning motion occurs along a dynamic circle that is constantly on the move in time and space.

For example, although the Earth rotates around the Sun, its orbit is not fixed in space but rather carves out a helical path with one helical turn completed each year— we are essentially getting a free ride in space courtesy of Earthship traveling a distance of nearly 600M miles each year.

Like Earth, other planets also trace out a similar helical trajectory as they orbit the Sun.

For its part, the Sun itself is not stationary but rather it is also on the move tracing out a helical path as it orbits the Milky Way—the galaxy of which our solar system is a part of.

In a similar fashion, the circle of human progress can also be envisioned to be traveling along a helical path in a manner akin to climbing a spiral staircase—such that each helical turn represents one complete circle.

In a nutshell, the oqual cycle posits that the progress of human civilization does not follow a linear course but rather it spirals (or spins) along an infinite helical path at a reciprocal velocity of 84 years per helical turn in sync with Uranus tracing out a helical path as it orbits the Sun (see Exhibit 3.8).

In mathematical terms, such a helix of radius r and pitch p within the framework of three-dimensional space (x,y,z) at time t can be described by the following set of parametric equations:

$$x[t] = r.\cos(t)$$
$$y[t] = r.\sin(t)$$
$$z[t] = (p/2\pi).t$$

wherein r can be envisioned as the radius of Uranus's orbit around the Sun, and p would then be the lateral distance that Uranus moves forward in space once every 84 years.

However, things begin to head south during the second half of the ride along the helical turn—being equivalent to traveling from one maximum (or the top of a mountain) to the next minimum (or the bottom of a valley) along a sinusoidal wave.

Put another way, the helix of human civilization may also be viewed as being amphipathic such that one side of the helix is the polar opposite of the other.

Thus, when traveling along the helix, humans find themselves at two extremes every 42 years as they switch their odyssey from the hydrophobic side of the helix to the hydrophilic or vice versa.

Such a mathematical model not only accounts for the waxing and waning of human civilization over the course of oqual cycle but also its overall progress in time and space a la movement of Uranus and other celestial bodies.

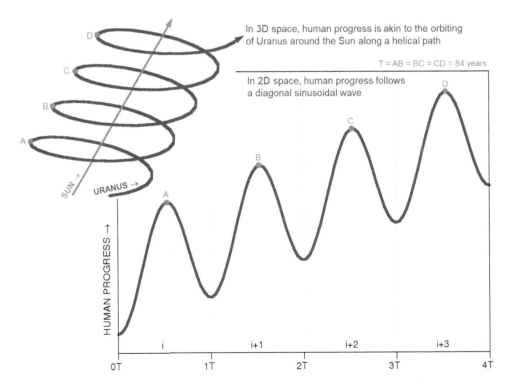

Exhibit 3.8 | While orbiting around the Sun, Uranus carves out a helical path with each turn of the helix completed over the course of 84 years. In a similar fashion, the oqual cycle plods along a three-dimensional (3D) helical path with each helical turn represented by one full sinusoidal turn in two-dimensional (2D) space such that human progress follows a diagonal wave in sync with the orbiting of the Uranus around the Sun in a helical manner. The letter i represents one full turn of oqual cycle. The points AB, BC, and CD are equi-temporal with T indicating the orbital period of Uranus.

|4| DOCTRINE

Ever since United States came into being as a nation in 1776, its leaders have been telling Americans that they are riding an express train supercharged with a double dose of capitalism-and-democracy and that their next stop is the idyllic land of nirvana (or utopia).

Yet, almost 250 years later, that dream of a utopian society run amok to the nth degree remains a fantasy at best.

American leaders have not been alone in spewing out such an asinine rhetoric over the past couple of centuries but they have also been joined by many leaders elsewhere around the world whose experiment to end bad times once-and-forever only exacerbated the pain and suffering of their people.

How can one oqualize (or rationalize) such razzmatazz that promised so much jazz but delivered little shazz?

Well, our past is the foundation upon which our present and future are built—the past acts rather like a rug under our feet which if pulled out not only makes us lose our balance but also our nuance.

In other words, the world leaders failed to pay heed to history.

They did not seem to realize that not only are we connected to our past via our DNA but also through our sociopolitical wave that has continued to ebb and flow since the beginning of times.

That is not only due to their own ignorance and hubris but, perhaps, more so from the ineptitude of seasoned historians—who for the most part have continued to deliver lessons of history as if it were a one-way train speeding along a linear track with no relation to its past.

Alas, it ain't.

Regrettably, it is not only the world leaders but even pundits-and-gurus remain ignorant of the cyclical nature of history and how it governs our lives due to their optimism bias—the misguided belief that tomorrow must necessarily be better than today and that bad times have long been put to the sword so as to never return again.

In particular, such idiocy runs deep in the media tail that wags the societal dog and therefore serves as a perpetual pill to keep the masses indoctrinated with their warped worldview rather than hard facts.

Being an optimist is a great virtue but being a realist is multiples greater.

Although many of my fellow Americans are renowned for seeing the glass half full, their ignorance and hubris also see no bounds.

While the embers of the decades-long self-destructive 9/11 Wars continue to rage to this day with the nation teetering on the brink of a looming bankruptcy coupled with social-and-moral decadence at home from soaring public debts through shrinking middle class to faltering infrastructure, so many Americans nevertheless do not shy away from prophesizing that the United States is destined for a utopian era waiting on the horizon with the promise of making its past look tame by comparison.

Little do they realize that the best days of America long took a trip down memory lane and what awaits them ahead is a rendezvous with destiny to pay for their excesses and imbalances amassed over the course of so many decades.

While one may be able to evade the scourge of courts due to what has essentially become an anarchic society wherein serial criminals are not only handsomely bred but also richly rewarded for their wicked acts, no one can keep the full force of the laws of nature at bay.

Nor does irrational optimism end well.

With World War III all but having begun with Russia's invasion of Ukraine in 2022, almost every form of frothy investment from bonds through stocks to real estate is set to plunge to ground zero over the next decade and, in doing so, leaving tens-of-millions of Americans poor and destitute.

Yet, so many fools continue to live in lalaland rather than face the hard reality as they plow ever more money into such bogus investments in the misguided belief that the worst is behind them and out of fear-of-missing-out (FOMO) the financial train ingenuously believed to be destined for Shangrila.

Nothing could be further from the truth.

In actuality, the financial train is headed to the fool's paradise and it is already too late for many to get off and avoid a terrible fate awaiting them ahead.

So what gives?

HUMAN PROGRESS WAXES AND WANES IN A CYCLICAL MANNER

On the basis of scientific reasoning and mathematical modeling of history over the past 600 years, the oqual cycle posits that human civilization seemingly undergoes a sweeping global reset once every 84 years on average in order to purge itself of a plethora of wrongdoings from the societal ills through excesses and imbalances to transgressions amassed over that multidecadal period.

Unfortunately, there is no free music as one must pay the piper.

Indeed, such a societal reboot (or revitalization) is typically accomplished through a global conflict with the potential to not only wreak havoc but also strike fear into the hearts and minds of people on an apocalyptic scale so that they can put their sociopolitical differences aside and come together for the common good of the world at large.

The oqual cycle therefore lends human society a subtle albeit deadly mechanism to break ties with its dysfunctional past in order to begin anew rather than being held hostage from moving forward under its own weight, or even worse, continue down the rabbit hole in perpetuity with the potential for self-destruction.

More specifically, the oqual cycle posits that the sociopolitical progress of human civilization does not follow a linear course but rather it waxes and wanes in a cyclical manner over a period of 84 years due to what appears to be its coupling with the orbiting of the second outermost planet Uranus around the Sun.

In an analogy with a pendulum, the progress of human civilization appears to swing (or oscillate) forth from one extreme to the other and then back again over a period of 84 years.

In an analogy with the trials and tribulations of a mouse with an average lifespan of one year, the oqual cycle is to humans what the annual cycle is to mice.

Just as mice remain clueless about annual seasonal changes affecting their lives so do humans with respect to the spell of Uranian seasons.

The ignorance of mice does not change the fact that the annual cycle substantially impacts their lives nor does our own ignorance about the dire spell of oqual cycle on our own lives.

How does the oqual cycle fit in with the Uranian seasons?

In sync with the changes in Uranian climate with respect to its southern pole, the oqual cycle is subdivided into a quartet of 21-year seasons chronologically dubbed spring, summer, autumn, and winter.

Simply put, the oqual cycle on Earth is perfectly synchronized with the Uranian year in that it begins with the southern spring and ends with the southern winter.

In terms of cyclical progress of human civilization over a period of 84 years, such a quartet of seasons can also be viewed as dawn (spring), sunrise (summer), sunset (autumn), and dusk (winter).

Needless to say, a 21-year timespan of oqual cycle equates to an oqual quarter and a 7-year period represents one oqual month.

In an alternative but a mutually-inclusive framework, the oqual cycle is envisioned as a doublet of two symmetrical (or antagonistic) halves: a constructive period marked by a rather upbeat zeitgeist (over the course of spring and summer) followed by a destructive spell during which the societal zeitgeist turns on its head (over the course of autumn and winter), with each lasting for some 42 years on average (see Exhibit 4.1).

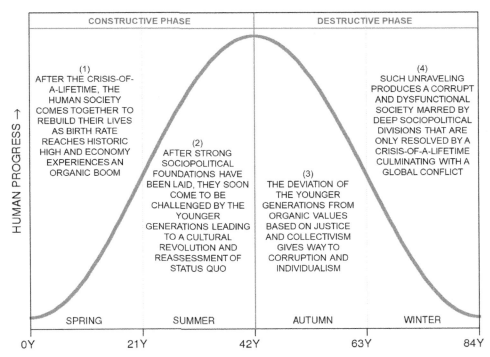

Exhibit 4.1 | The oqual cycle posits that the progress of human civilization ebbs and flows in a sinusoidal manner over a period of 84 years (Y) in a manner akin to the waxing and waning of the moon over the course of a lunar month. Every 84 years on average, such an oqual cycle begins with a honeymoon spearheaded by a new sociopolitical order and ends with a crisis-of-a-lifetime that brings about a global conflict so as to break ties with the old-and-degenerate system. In doing so, the oqual cycle ushers in a new dawn of hope and prosperity in a manner similar to the start of a new day or new year.

In other words, human progress waxes over the first half of oqual cycle to reach a zenith and then wanes during the second half to hit a nadir in a sinusoidal manner reminiscent of the waxing and waning of the Moon over the course of a lunar month.

Why does human progress wax and wane over the course of oqual cycle?

When human society hits a nadir (or crisis-of-a-lifetime) in the face of sociopolitical upheaval having reached a climax as the oqual cycle draws to a close, it becomes boxed-cornered-and-trapped with no way out.

Paradoxically, such a checkmate serves as a blessing-in-disguise to revitalize human society and provide it with a renewed vigor to rebuild a just sociopolitical system that seemingly works for most people as it reaches its zenith during the first half of oqual cycle before it turns on its head.

For example, during the first half (1955-1996) of the current oquannium (1955-2038), the sociopolitical temperature was by-and-large relatively healthy across much of the globe with occasional bouts of sociopolitical crisis that were largely contained within the national or regional borders rather than becoming sticky so as to draw the whole world into a quandary.

Today, long gone are those good old days as we find ourselves in the midst of what appears to be not only a concerted and synchronized sociopolitical upheaval unfolding across the globe but that has also continued to plunge humanity into an ever-deepening canyon with the passing of each year since the onset of the second half (1997-2038) of the current oquannium (1955-2038).

In a manner similar to the good old days of our own lives during the first half (1955-1996) of the current and seventh oquannium (1955-2038), a similar zeitgeist of relative calm and prosperity also panned out during the first half (1871-1912) of the previous and sixth oquannium (1871-1954), yet the second half (1913-1954) was mired in utter sociopolitical crises and deadly conflicts as epitomized by the quartet of World War I (1914-1918), Influenza Pandemic (1918-1920), Great Depression (1929-1939), and World War II (1939-1945).

Likewise, the first half (1787-1828) of the fifth oquannium (1787-1870) bore witness to a period of relative harmony, whereas the second half (1829-1870) saw the world hit a low yet again through sociopolitical upheavals and conflicts such as the Mexican-American War (1846-1848), the European Revolutions (1848-1849), the Crimean War (1853-1856) between Russia and Turkiye, the Indian Mutiny (1857) against the British colonialists, the American Civil War (1861-1865), and the Franco-Mexican War (1861-1867).

Long story short, humanity has consistently faced a multidecadal period of trials and tribulations during the second half of every qual cycle since the birth of Modern Age in 1451.

On the other hand, the first half of oqual cycle has by and large equated to a period of relative peace and prosperity.

What sociopolitical forces cooperate to produce the rather happy times during the first half of oqual cycle?

The relatively calm and prosperous 42-year period over the course of the first half of oqual cycle is powered by the steady rise of a myriad of progressive sociopolitical forces such as morality, peace, collectivism, globalism, entrepreneurship, moderation, transparency, nonpartisanship, ethnic harmony, baby boom, economic well-being, and institutional trust.

To add icing on the cake, such progressive forces act in a positively-cooperative (or synergistic) manner in that their combined output is much more productive than the sum of their individual parts—their concerted action engineers a sociopolitical system spearheaded by a relatively healthy dose of prosperity enjoyed by the masses rather than restricted to a small minority of wealthy.

In particular, the deluge of such sociopolitical tailwinds descending upon our civilization during the first half of oqual cycle is further inundated with ground-breaking scientific discoveries and technological advances that are often viewed in hindsight as among the greatest of all time.

For example, what came to be known as the Golden Age in America—an era that bore witness to the discoveries of DNA double-helix (1953) and protein structure (1957) coupled with NASA's moon landing (1969), the development of internet's precursor Arpanet (1969), and Alto's launch of first-ever GUI-based personal computer (1973)—largely overlapped with the oqual spring (1955-1975) of the current and seventh oquannium (1955-2038).

Likewise, the oqual spring (1871-1891) of the previous and sixth oquannium (1871-1954) coincided with the so-called Gilded Age in America, the Late Victorian Era in Britain, and La Belle Époque in France—an era that attested to the development of typewriter (1868), the discovery of DNA (1869), and the opening of Suez Canal (1869) to add to the launch of telephone (1876), light bulb (1879), gasoline car (1886), movie camera (1891), and air conditioner (1902).

On the same token, the oqual spring (1787-1807) of the fifth oquannium (1787-1870) would usher in a new economic system on American soil termed Market Economy wherein production of goods and services were to be solely driven by the supply-demand equilibria buttressed by corporate competition without interference from any external forces—it is indeed no coincidence that the engine of modern capitalism in the form of New York Stock Exchange came into being in 1792 at the dawn of the fifth oqual cycle to add to a number of other ground-breaking innovations such as the launch of the optical telegraph (1792), the development of maiden vaccine against the smallpox virus (1796), the birth of steam train (1812), and the debut of photographic camera (1816).

While scientific discoveries and technological advances are also aplenty during the second half of oqual cycle, their predominantly applied-and-commercial nature pales in comparison to the largely fundamental-and-seminal breakthroughs made during the first half.

However, all good things eventually come to an end due to what appears to be a universal rhythm that apparently transcends the underpinnings of every form of matter and energy in nature.

Admittedly, the rather favorable sociopolitical forces essential for the maintenance and integrity of overall prosperity of a society begin to wane and head south as the oqual cycle approaches its summit (or turning point) after what is often viewed in the rearview mirror as a nostalgic period of some 42 years.

Why do the rather good times of the first half of oqual cycle eventually come to an end?

Over the rather long 42-year constructive phase of relative peace and harmony enjoyed over the course of the first half of oqual cycle, people's memories of hard times endured during the nadir at the dusk of previous oqual cycle largely become erased, or rather, they brush aside lessons of history in the tainted belief that it would never repeat.

Such a toxic combo of ignorance and hubris coupled with prosperity not only plants a false sense of complacency but also democratizes a culture of living beyond means, and in doing so, it makes younger generations become self-indulgent and hedonistic such that they feel that good times will perhaps never end but they always do.

One indeed cannot have the cake and eat it too!

The resulting triumph of hedonism over collectivism fuels the resurgence of a plethora of regressive sociopolitical forces such as immorality, conflict, individualism, populism, fraud, debt, corruption, partisanship, xenophobia, baby bust, wealth polarization, and institutional distrust.

To add gasoline to fire, such regressive forces act in a negatively-cooperative (or counter-synergistic) manner in that their combined output is much more toxic than the sum of their individual parts—their concerted action produces a sociopolitical system that is heavily rigged in favor of a small minority of wealthy wherein the masses become exploited rather than being justly rewarded for their proportional contributions to the society.

While the first half of oqual cycle is underscored by a bucketload of progressive forces acting in a concerted fashion to outweigh the malaise of regressive forces, the balance of power turns on its head during the second half when the regressive forces conspire to not only neutralize but also override the overpowering weight of their better counterparts (see Exhibit 4.2).

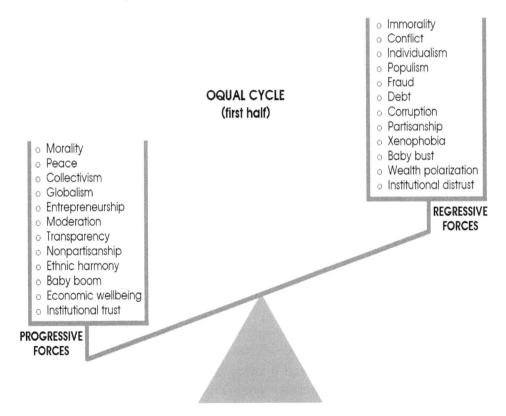

Exhibit 4.2 | The first half of oqual cycle is underscored by progressive forces acting in a concerted fashion to outweigh the malaise of regressive forces. The balance of power however turns on its head during the second half when the regressive forces conspire to not only neutralize but also override the overpowering weight of their better counterparts.

Indeed, during the second half of oqual cycle, greed mongers and wicked souls within the human society act in a concerted fashion to not only hijack the system so as to funnel resources away from the masses toward a small minority of wealthy and elite but they also set about pulverizing moral values that had served as the bedrock of our civilization during the first half.

In other words, our sociopolitical system is pushed to its limit with all levers of control being turned to full throttle with self-destruction all but guaranteed.

For example, much of the globe has been bedeviled by an ever-deepening canyon of sociopolitical upheaval with each passing year since the outset of the second half (1997-2038) of the current oquannium (1955-2038) as summed up below in a chronological order:

1) NATO Expansion (1999-date)
2) Consumption Mania (2000-date)
3) 9/11 Wars (2001-2021)
4) Climate Propaganda (2006-date)
5) Global Financial Crisis (2007-2008)
6) Money Printing (2008-date)
7) Debt Mania (2008-date)
8) Cultural Dysphoria (2008-date)
9) Arab Spring (2010-2012)
10) Libyan Civil War (2011-date)
11) Syrian Civil War (2011-date)
12) Coronavirus Pandemic (2019-2023)
13) Consumer Price Inflation (2021-date)
14) Russia-Ukraine War (2022-date)

Add to such sociopolitical crises the fact that our society is also being peppered by disruptive forces from both the far-left and the far-right as the current oqual cycle nears its end.

On the far-left, the leaders and their herd muddy the societal waters through what has come to be dubbed "Wokeism"—a deeply-polarizing and disruptive ideology that claims to be aware of what it perceives to be sociopolitical prejudices, injustices, and inequalities endemic to human society as embodied in the so-called "critical race theory".

On the far-right, the leaders up the ante by gaslighting the majority into believing that they are the victims of the minority in order to win their votes rather than addressing real-life problems—such a divisive ideology powered in no uncertain terms by demagoguery is further exacerbated by right-wing politics emerging across the globe.

As if such a confluence of rightwing polarizing politics and leftwing propaganda does not spark a crisis vying to hold its own, Mother Nature also gets in on the act as it appears to reserve the worst of its scourge on humanity by virtue of its ability to unleash a barrage of natural disasters just when we are at our worst and least prepared during the second half of oqual cycle.

Such synergism between Mother Nature and humanity's unspectacular unraveling plunge the society into an even deeper sociopolitical crisis.

For example, the second half (1997-2038) of the current oquannium (1955-2038) has hitherto witnessed some of the most crippling natural calamities of our lifetime such as the 2004 Indian Ocean Tsunami, the 2005 Kashmir Earthquake, the 2008 Sichuan Earthquake, the 2010 Haiti Earthquake, the 2011 Japanese Tsunami, the 2019 Coronavirus Pandemic, and the 2023 Turkiye Earthquake.

In a similar manner, the second half (1913-1954) of the previous and sixth oquannium (1871-1954) was marred by the 1918 Influenza Pandemic across the globe, the 1920 Haiyuan Earthquake in China, the 1923 Kanto Earthquake in Japan, the 1934 Dust Bowl over North America, the 1935 Quetta Earthquake in Pakistan, and the 1948 Ashgabat Earthquake in Turkmenistan.

Likewise, during the second half (1829-1870) of the fifth oquannium (1787-1870), the world was plagued by some of the worst natural disasters recorded in recent memory such as the 1833 Sumatra Tsunami in Indonesia, the 1846 Third Cholera Pandemic across the globe, and the 1868 Arica Earthquake in Chile.

Against the backdrop of such natural calamities coupled with sociopolitical upheaval showing no signs of easing, it is therefore hardly surprising that the second half of oqual cycle spanning a 42-year destructive phase culminates with an utterly dysfunctional society marred by systemic corruption and incompetence at all levels.

The resulting dire societal straits trigger a crisis-of-a-lifetime that paves the way for the dismantling of the old-and-degenerate system through a global conflict of epic proportions so as to usher in a nouveau sociopolitical order.

Henceforth, the oqual cycle begins all over again after having experienced two consecutive bouts of construction followed by destruction, with each lasting for some 42 years on average.

With each essentially mirroring the other, such a pair of constructive-destructive stages can also be viewed as an 84-year symmetrical dyad of peace-crisis, growth-decay, boom-bust, upturn-downturn, uphill-downhill, ascendance-descendance, integration-disintegration, progression-regression, winding-unwinding, folding-unfolding, coupling-uncoupling, bonding-unbonding, fusion-fission, nucleation-atomization, and so forth.

Is oqual cycle akin to climbing and descending a mountain then?

HUMAN PROGRESS IS AKIN TO TRAVERSING THROUGH A SERIES OF MOUNTAINS AND VALLEYS

When viewed through the prism of oqual cycle, it seems that human progress is akin to climbing and descending a mountain over a period of 84 years, and then repeating the whole process all over again.

Over the course of an oqual cycle, we seemingly climb uphill to reach the summit during the first 42 years followed by rolling downhill to reach the valley beneath over the next 42 years (see Exhibit 4.3).

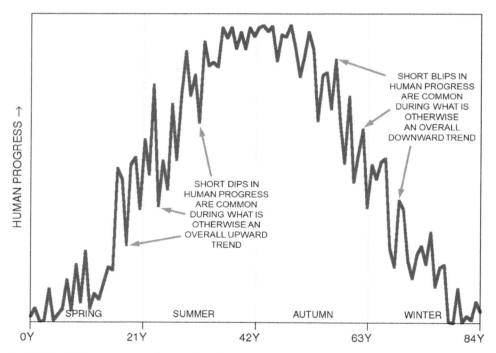

Exhibit 4.3 | The oqual cycle can be viewed as a mountain punctuated with a rugged landscape on each side. Even during the first half epitomized by an overall prosperity among the masses, the human civilization nevertheless encounters temporal bouts of setbacks. Likewise, short but unsustainable spells of happy times are also enjoyed during the second half when the overall sociopolitical mood is on the decline.

However, it is important to keep in mind that neither climbing uphill during the first half of oqual cycle nor rolling downhill during the second half encounters a smooth journey.

Rather, each stage is punctuated with a rough (or rugged) landscape that temporarily involves falling into a spate of local minima (or gorges) followed by rising up the local maxima (or ridges) as the oqual cycle continues the journey either uphill or downhill.

In other words, even during what is overall a time of sustained growth and prosperity for the masses while climbing uphill, human civilization nevertheless encounters occasional setbacks and crises though they rarely metastasize beyond national or regional borders.

In a similar manner, during what is overall a time of stagnation and regression while rolling downhill, human civilization nonetheless experiences short bursts of rapid growth and innovation though their benefits rarely trickle down to the masses.

Do we plant our own downfall after reaching the summit?

When viewing the sphere of our civilization from a wider angle, it seems that humans are in fact the victims of their own success—the fallout from the very forces that catapult them to the summit of the oqual mountain during the first half seemingly comes back to haunt them or becomes somewhat of a drag on their checkered progress during the second half.

Put another way, the seeds of our downfall in the second half of oqual cycle are actually planted during the first half—the first half is essentially a double-edged sword in that the very forces that conspire to produce a relatively calm and prosperous period do so with a sizeable amount of undesirable secondary effects that only come into play as we enter the second half.

Thus, the hard times encountered during the second half could also be viewed as a by-product of our earlier actions during the first half.

For example, new technologies such as phone, television, refrigerator, car, and air conditioner which had been an exclusive domain of the wealthy and elite prior to World War II (1939-1945) became democratized by leaps-and-bounds across much of the Western world just as the first half (1955-1996) of the current oquannium (1955-2038) kicked off.

Such a paradigm shift in the sociopolitical order during the second half of the 20th century was made possible due to the redirection of mass production from military arsenal to consumer goods and services as World War II drew to a close—thereby fueling an unprecedented economic boom that created high-paying jobs en masse and brought prosperity to virtually every corner of America in what would come to be called America's Golden Age (1950-1970).

However, such an economic boom also created a consumer culture as a by-product that would not only make the younger generations adopt a reckless lifestyle of living beyond their means but would also put their health and that of their environment in peril.

Admittedly, the unprecedented rise in ailments from diabetes through cancer to cardiovascular disease over the past half-a-century-or-so is largely a making of our own despicable behavior from abusing carcinogen-laden cosmetics through consuming processed foods to a sedentary lifestyle befitting a couch potato.

Likewise, the scientific and technological breakthroughs during the first half (1955-1996) of the current oquannium (1955-2038) also laid the foundations for the manufacturing of synthetic drugs en masse with the result that the perpetual use of such toxins has left our precarious bodies on the brink of collapse—thanks to modern-day profit-driven bogus medical practices that seem to have a nasty drug for every cure from children to the elderly without properly warning the public of their long-term devastating effects, thereby sucking them into a vicious cycle of drug dependency.

Dirven by the capitalist propaganda to make money by any means possible, there is now a drug for everything to decimate the health of the unsuspecting hoi polloi.

There is a drug to stimulate your appetite, another one to suppress it, yet another one to push your stools out, and then the magic pill that puts you to sleep, and then there is another silver bullet at your disposal to wake you up.

And that is before even mentioning a plethora of nasty compounds being marketed to help the masses focus on their studies, boost intelligence, avoid procrastination, keep anxiety at bay, and even make them happy.

Yet, drugs do far more harm to our bodies in that for every bodily function that they purportedly resolve, they create another ten problems.

Notably, a quantum leap in the chemical synthesis of drugs during the second half of the 20th century has also led to mass production of all sorts of recreational drugs today—the widespread abuse of such harmful substances not only causes addiction but also continues to destroy the lives of addicts and their families on an unprecedented scale.

Today, the opioid crisis worldwide may represent the tip of the iceberg of young generations having lost zest for life but the seeds of their downfall were planted many decades earlier during a time of relative peace and harmony.

It is not just the intoxication of our bodies that is the disorder of the day but our despicable behaviors have also left our environment on the brink of collapse thanks in large part to today's consumer culture that in no small part has been powered by the scientific and technological breakthroughs made during the first half (1955-1996) of the current oquannium (1955-2038).

SOCIOPOLITICAL UPHEAVAL IS A HALLMARK OF THE SECOND HALF OF OQUAL CYCLE

According to Murphy's law, anything that can go wrong will go wrong. While that law remains deeply controversial, its validity is best demonstrated during times of sociopolitical crisis that befalls humanity during the second half of oqual cycle.

Indeed, being in the midst of the second half (1997-2038) of the current oquannium (1955-2038), most of us would wholeheartedly bear testimony to such a bedlam firsthand.

What were once relatively good old days during the second half of the 20th century came to an abrupt end at the outset of 21st century across much of the globe just as the current oquannium (1955-2038) entered its second half—a 42-year period that nominally kicked off in 1997 though the sparks did not go off until the hijacked planes struck America on 2001/09/11.

To put this into the context of the annual cycle, the beginning-in-earnest of the second half of the current oqual cycle in 2001 in lieu of 1997 would be akin to a storm arriving about a fortnight later than expected.

Witnessed firsthand as I saw unprecedented plumes of smoke billowing over Downtown Manhattan along with the rising sun from the rather comfort of a high-rise building in Midtown, that fateful day on 9/11 marked a watershed that signaled the arrival-in-earnest of a 42-year tumultuous period across the globe as it brought virtually every nation-on-earth to conform to a new normal that has stuck with us ever since.

Yet, each one of the four American presidents to have been at the helm since 9/11 did not shy away from reassuring the faithful at home and abroad with a rather absurd message that America's best days were yet to come—even when the naked truth has been the diametric opposite all along.

Worse yet, in the aftermath of 9/11 attacks, many worshippers of capitalism across America rekindled the fairytale of a utopian era waiting on the horizon with the promise of making America's past look tame by comparison—even if that came at the expense of preemptively annihilating millions of innocent souls across the globe and destroying other nations with impunity.

To the contrary, America has been steadily rolling downhill ever since 9/11 though still quite a distance away from reaching a deep canyon with a rock and a hard place anxiously waiting below for the catch-of-a-lifetime.

Tellingly, America's spectacular fall from grace has also wrapped virtually every other nation-of-the-world into a sociopolitical quagmire from where all roads lead to a deep canyon.

Although widely-touted as a leader of the free world during much of the 20th century, America has been acting more like a ringleader of the mafia since 9/11.

While the list of America's crimes over the past several decades is exhaustive, it can be summed up under the following two major points:

1) Using 9/11 attacks as a pretense and under the false guise of weapons of mass destruction being developed by Iraq, America and its NATO poodles not only razed to ground but also created chaos and power vacuum across much of the Middle East through waging unethical-illegal-and-immoral decades-long wars in the name of democracy and freedom even though the hidden propaganda was to exercise America's might and subdue weaker nations harboring natural resources, strategic importance, or posing threat to the petrodollar; and

2) Robbing the economic prosperity of future generations of Americans through printing trillions of dollars in a reckless manner and borrowing to the hilt to finance the unnecessary 9/11 Wars as well as to promote an irresponsible and immoral culture of living beyond means that has not only left the American society teetering on the ropes but also the planet earth—overconsumption is largely a making of America and its brand of sick capitalism that has infected virtually every other nation-on-earth with no signs of cresting.

What used to be the good-old-shiny-happy days for much of the second half of the 20th century indeed appear to have evaporated forever in the aftermath of 9/11 just as they did some 84 years earlier with the onset of World War I in 1914.

In line with the dire spell of oqual cycle, that despicable period coincided with the second half (1913-1954) of the previous and sixth oquannium (1871-1954).

Admittedly, those earlier times witnessed two world wars, an economic depression, extreme poverty, resurgence of xenophobia, soaring public debts, widening wealth gap, shrinking middle class, growing sociopolitical partisanship, rise of populism, metastasis of Ponzism, and plummeting trust of governments in America and across much of the globe.

That period also witnessed the borders of so many nations redrawn as well as the birth of new nations on an unprecedented scale from Gandhi's India (1947) and Jinnah's Pakistan (1947) to Ben-Gurion's Israel (1948) and Mao's China (1949).

On the other hand, the 1920s saw an exponential rise and spread of Ponzism—the widespread emergence of a paraphernalia of get-rich-quick and pump-and-dump schemes unleashed by the likes of fraudsters, swindlers, and con-artists whose concerted actions planted the seeds for the 1929 historic crash of the stock market that would subsequently lead to the Great Depression (1929-1939) followed by World War II (1939-1945).

Some 84 years later, Ponzism has once again grown into an 800-pound gorilla since the onset of the second half (1997-2038) of the current and seventh oquannium (1955-2038)—such a fraudulent culture has hitherto caused the popping of the 2000 Dotcom Bubble and the 2007 Housing Bubble.

In the wake of the 2019 Coronavirus Pandemic, Ponzism has been run amok to the quartic power in the form of cryptos, non-fungible tokens (NFTs), special purpose acquisition companies (SPACs), and meme stocks—the stocks of virtually bankrupt and zombie companies heavily traded on the market and catapulted to the sky, merely due to their popularity on social media rather than their corporate fundamentals, only for them to come back crashing to earth and leaving fools holding the bag.

Indeed, such Ponzi schemes not only propelled the stock markets but also the housing markets around the globe to become extremely frothy and bubblicious in 2021—a crash-of-a-lifetime is thus once again on the cards, and like the 1929 crash, it will also leave millions of fools-and-horses without clothes.

Regrettably, such reckless behavior on the part of humanity is nothing short of signs of terrible times on the horizon threatening to upend the very fabric of society to which we have become accustomed to in our lives.

Of course, such a familiar movie has been playing out during the second half of every oqual cycle since the beginning of times.

One notable case from these earlier times is the launch of railway transport during the early 19th century.

While the first half (1787-1828) of the fifth oquannium (1787-1870) saw the launch of railway transport across many parts of Europe and North America, the second half (1829-1870) provided an opportunity for the Ponzi schemes to capitalize on its growing popularity in the United Kingdom in what came to be known as the 1846 Railway Mania—fraudsters scammed millions of people of their life-savings through selling shares of bogus companies that would claim to build new railway lines even though they only existed on paper a la SPACs of today.

Being in the midst of the second half (1997-2038) of the current oquannium (1955-2038), no one should therefore be surprised that a similar drama of Ponzi schemes and sociopolitical chaos is being played out once again in plain sight.

In disguise of the Oracle of Omaha Warren Buffett, only when the tide goes out does one get to see those who are skinny-dipping (or swimming naked).

As the oqual cycle draws to a close, the tide does indeed go out on such fraudsters and their accomplices leaving them not only embarrassed and humiliated but also behind bars for good.

Such a dire fate does not only await individuals with a bad karma but also nations that have continued to transgress unabated over the course of oqual cycle.

While America has been by far the largest perpetrator of transgressions over the past several decades, its allies in Asia and Europe have also closely followed in its dirty footsteps.

The likes of Japan, United Kingdom, and the European Union have practically destroyed their economies—and hence sociopolitical homeostasis—through aggressive money printing that began almost in concurrence with the onset of the second half (1997-2038) of the current oquannium (1955-2038).

While the currencies of other nations by-and-large carry little value outside their borders, their respective leaders have nevertheless been tearing down their rather healthy sociopolitical strata over the past couple of decades through taking on excessive debt so as to fuel the addiction of their people rapidly becoming accustomed to being provided for rather than being able to stand on their own feet a la their parents and grandparents before them.

Today, it is therefore no coincidence that virtually every nation-of-the-world has hit an abyss—the like of which we have not seen in a lifetime—as viewed through virtually every angle from economic well-being to sociopolitical stability.

With the ongoing sociopolitical upheaval around the world having reached a tipping point and rapidly approaching a deep canyon, there is simply going to be no soft landing.

Rather, when push comes to shove, the only viable solution is to completely do away with the old system and begin anew.

Tellingly, a new dawn of good-old-shiny-happy days is on the horizon and will likely arrive some time during the 2030s in a manner akin to the beginning of relatively prosperous times during the 1950s, 1870s, and 1790s savored on American soil and across much of the globe.

However, the ongoing sociopolitical upheaval will get multiples worse over the next decade or so before we see the light at the end of the oqual tunnel.

In other words, the human society not only finds itself in a bind but has also been rolling downhill since the outset of 21st century and it will continue to do so for at least another decade before it reverses course and begins to climb uphill once again with a renewed vigor just as it did some 84 years ago during the 1950s.

In particular, the decade centered on annus horribilis (2028) of the current oquannium (1955-2038) does not bear good omens as it will be paralyzed by a global conflict of epic proportions due to the convergence and resurgence of so many regressive sociopolitical forces such as debt, populism, corruption, xenophobia, partisanship, wealth gap, and dysfunctional governments.

While a global conflict is not absolutely necessary to bringing about such a reset every 84 years, it is all but obligatory.

WHY A GLOBAL CONFLICT IS A PREREQUISITE TO BRING THE ONGOING SOCIOPOLITICAL UPHEAVAL AROUND THE GLOBE TO AN END

Few would disagree that the current sociopolitical system around the globe has hit a nadir like never before in our lives.

Not only has it become inundated with swamp from left-and-right but it is also broken down to bare bones such that it cannot be fixed but rather it needs to be wholly replaced by a new system with the mandate to begin anew at the expense of dismantling corrupt and dysfunctional institutions.

In other words, when the sociopolitical system hits such a low, it is time to drain the swamp.

In particular, such a swamp spearheaded by deep societal rifts serves as a thermodynamic bottleneck making it energetically unfavorable for people on opposite sides of the sociopolitical spectrum to come to a consensus and agree to work together.

That is until they fall into an abyss-of-a-lifetime.

Simply put, when people hit their lowest point, only then are they open to working together so as to usher in the greatest change (or revolution) in their sociopolitical system.

History has shown time and again that such a nadir on average occurs once in a lifetime, or once every 84 years, as the sociopolitical upheaval that takes hold during the second half of oqual cycle reaches a tipping point and, in doing so, triggers a global conflict of epic proportions so as to acquiesce to a new dawn of hope and prosperity.

As the saying goes, there is no rose without a thorn.

Admittedly, a large-scale global conflict with the potential to not only wreak havoc on an astronomical scale but also strike terror into the hearts and minds of people appears to be a prerequisite for breaking ties with our past and old traditions so as to revitalize human society and usher in a brighter tomorrow.

Without such a real-life horror show, people on opposite sides of the sociopolitical spectrum refuse to see eye-to-eye in order to come to a consensus necessary to rid the society of its wrongdoings amassed over the course of oqual cycle.

In other words, only under such an apocalyptic scenario, people put their differences aside and come together for a common cause that involves rebooting their society and beginning anew.

More specifically, a global conflict revitalizes the human society by leaps and bounds via a three-pronged mechanism as follows:

1) **Constructive fear**—The global conflict strikes fear into the hearts and minds of people so that they can put their differences aside and come to a consensus necessary to dismantle old-and-dysfunctional institutions

and replace them with new ones better suited for new times. For example, social security benefits to take care of people from the cradle to the grave irrespective of their contributions to the society in America and across much of the Western world began on either side of World War II (1939-1945). In fact, revolutionary institutions such as America's Social Security Administration (1935), United Nations (1945), UK National Insurance Act (1946), UK National Assistance Act (1948), UK National Health Service (1948), and North Atlantic Treaty Organization (1949) only came into being during the crisis-of-a-lifetime as the previous oquannium (1871-1954) headed for the exit. Others such as European Union (1957), Federal Aviation Administration (1958), National Aeronautics and Space Administration (1958) would follow hot on the heels of the nominal start of the current oquannium (1955-2038). Needless to say, a similar roster of revolutionary institutions also took hold at the cusp of previous oqual cycles. Likewise, the looming World War III will provide a perfect backdrop to dismantle so many failed experiments such as social-welfare programs across much of the Western world that have brought it down to its knees. Only under the veneer of such an apocalyptic-esque scenario will the Western governments become emboldened to axe such free handouts that have contributed to their downfall.

2) **Technological renaissance**—The global conflict causes a large-scale destruction of infrastructure with the potential to turn cities renowned for their hustle-and-bustle into ghost towns. While this may seem like a setback at first sight, it actually serves to create new opportunities for mass employment, widespread entrepreneurship, and modernization of industry as rebuilding from ashes gets underway. Thus, new technologies waiting on the fringes of the society quickly move to the center of our civilization and become the toast of the town. It seems as if the global conflict helps to quickly clear out old technologies and traditions lest they strangulate human civilization through their ability to hold us hostage from moving forward to a new experiment. In the aftermath of World War II (1939-1945), the US government enacted the so-called Marshall Plan (1948) so as to provide war-torn Europe with a massive financial aid to help it not only get back on its feet once more but also do so with a vengeance. At home on American soil, a quantum leap in the production of goods and services due to the availability of new technologies catapulted the US economy to the moon in the post-WWII era though with the false perception that the good times were perhaps never going to end. Notably, new technologies such as phone, television,

refrigerator, car, and air conditioner, which had been an exclusive domain of the wealthy and elite prior to World War II quickly became democratized across much of the Western world as the previous oquannium (1871-1954) reached its climax. Likewise, similar economic booms and rapid democratization of new technologies have also been witnessed at the transition of previous oqual cycles. With the threat of World War III looming large over our head and shoulders, old technologies are already being cleared out and making way for new ones to take their place from how we work, how we socialize, how we conduct business, and so forth. Expect new technologies such as digital currencies, autonomous cars, and delivery robots to become a-dime-a-dozen in about a decade or so on the other side of World War III.

3) **Survival of the fittest**—As cruel as the laws of nature may seem, they are nevertheless unavoidable due to biology's inherent drive for the survival of the fittest at the expense of the weak. It seems that not only a global conflict but even regional and civil wars are a product of biology designed to weed out the weak so as to concentrate limited resources for the betterment of the fittest. It may come as a surprise to witness the murder of the weaker cub by their stronger sibling while the mother lioness not only sits by quietly but also makes no attempt to intervene so as to strike a truce between her two warring offspring unless one understands the ruthless power of biology. Unfortunately, a global conflict appears to be a biological mechanism that keeps human population in check through staging a large-scale destruction of human life every 84 years on average either through a direct hit or indirectly via destroying essential supply lines necessary for survival. Since such a mass execution disproportionately affects the weak who in the eyes of biology are unnecessarily sucking resources away from the more competitive individuals and becoming a burden on the society, it exquisitely serves its purpose in ensuring the survival of the fittest. By a conservative estimate, the three major calamities of the second half (1913-1954) of the previous oquannium (1871-1954) in the form of World War I (1914-1918), the Influenza Pandemic (1918-1920), and World War II (1939-1945) together reduced the then global population of around 2000M by at least 10%. Given that the global population has exponentially exploded since the end of WWII to 8000M today, the looming WWIII bears the potential to make its predecessor look like a dress rehearsal as we approach the interface of the current (1954-2038) and next (2039-2122) oquannia.

OQUAL CYCLE REPRESENTS A ROSETTA STONE OF HUMAN CIVILIZATION

History tells us that humans boast a dubious reputation of burning themselves down and then rising from the ashes to start all over again.

The oqual cycle argues that such a process of purification (or regeneration) does not occur randomly but rather in an orderly and cyclical manner over a period of 84 years on average.

While the cyclical nature of human civilization is hardy a breaking news (see Exhibit 4.4), a number of characteristics nevertheless set the oqual cycle apart from the previous models as summarized below:

1) It has a fixed periodicity of exactly 84 years.
2) It is globally synchronized in that the trials and tribulations of human society across the globe occur in lockstep with each other.
3) It is universal in that it envisions almost every facet of human civilization from politics through economy to climate to oscillate in a synchronized manner over a period of 84 years.
4) It is based on a systematic calendar synchronized with the Uranian year beginning with the southern spring and ending with the southern winter.

Simply put, the oqual cycle not only supersedes the previous models but it also appears to be a lower-order harmonic of the daily and annual cycles.

Nevertheless, credit must be given where credit is due for it is the painstaking work of previous authors whose provocative models laid the foundation for the development of the theory of oqual cycle.

Notably, the oqual cycle is not set in stone in a manner akin to the annual cycle but rather its dynamics are highly fluid and malleable with respect to the recurrence of eerily-similar events spaced apart by some 84 years.

For example, the worst storm of an annual winter does not necessarily arrive in January or February in the northern hemisphere but it may also stop us in our tracks as early as December in one year or as late as March in the following year.

In a similar manner, the archetypal (or quintessential) events within an oqual cycle may also occur at the beginning of a season or toward the end.

Just as the worst winter storms of two consecutive years may be bifurcated by as little as 9 months to as much as 15 months (12 ± 3 months), the global conflicts (or hegemonic wars) preceding the reset of sociopolitical order (or other archetypal events) may also be separated by as little as 63 years to as much as 105 years (84 ± 21 years) between two consecutive oqual cycles—though they usually occur within a much narrower window of between 77 to 91 years (84 ± 7 years).

	The Oqual Cycle [This Book]	Ages of Discord [3]	The Fourth Turning [2]	Long Cycles in World Politics [1]
First Published	2023	2016	1997	1987
Historical Window	1400-2023	1700-2016	1500-1997	1500-1987
Quantitative Data	Yes	Yes	No	No
Periodicity	84 years	150-200 years	80-100 years	80-120 years
Periodicity Fixed	Yes	No	No	No
Systematic Calendar	Yes	No	No	No
Previous Cycle	1871-1954	1780-1919	1866-1945	1900-??
Current Cycle	1955-2038	1920-??	1946-??	??
Next Cycle	2039-2122	??	??	??
Geographical Region	Global	United States	United States	Global
Global Synchronization	Yes	No	No	No
Celestial Orchestrator	Uranus	None	None	None
Societal Domains	Universal	Sociopolitical History	Sociopolitical History	Sociopolitical History
Author Name	Amjad Farooq	Peter Turchin	William Strauss and Neil Howe	George Modelski
Author Background	Biophysicist and Polymath	Ecologist and Anthropologist	Historian (WS) Historian (NH)	Political Scientist
Author Nationality	Pakistani-British-American	Russian-American	American (WS) American (NH)	Polish-American
Author Lifespan	1971-date	1957-date	1947-2007 (WS) 1951-date (NH)	1926-2014

Exhibit 4.4 | Comparison between The Oqual Cycle and previous models proposed to account for the cyclical nature of human civilization. Note that The Oqual Cycle not only stands out in the crowd but it is also universal in that almost every facet of human civilization from politics through culture and economy to climate is envisioned to oscillate in a synchronized manner over a period of 84 years in lockstep with the Uranian year beginning with the southern spring and ending with the southern winter.

However, just as the annual cycle on average occurs over 365 days, the oqual cycle does so over an average period of 84 years.

Likewise, just as some annual winters are relatively mild and pass by quietly, the dusk (or winter) of one oqual cycle may seamlessly blend into the dawn (or spring) of the next without too much drama and chaos on display.

Like annual winters which can be relatively mild or extremely severe, not all oqual cycles are created equal either—some end with an apocalyptic-esque bang while others seamlessly transition from one cycle to the next depending on the magnitude and intensity (or amplitude) of wrongdoings amassed over the course of the cycle (see Exhibit 4.5).

The fact that the oqual cycle may end with a quasi-apocalypse or transition from one cycle to the next in a somewhat subtle manner could explain why our sociopolitical system is proposed to undergo a global reset over a period roughly spanning the length of almost two oqual cycles according to the 2016 book titled "Ages of Discord" by Peter Turchin [3].

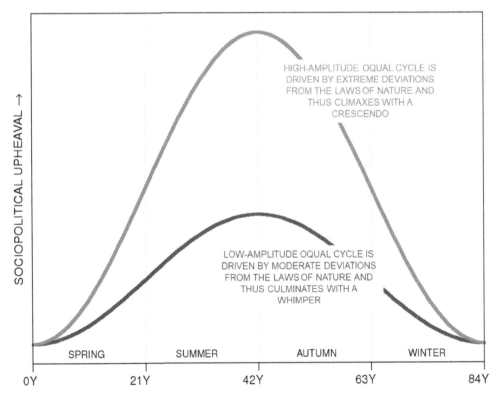

Exhibit 4.5 | Not all oqual cycles are created equal. Depending on the amplitude of sociopolitical upheaval, the oqual cycle may end with a crescendo or a whimper.

Notwithstanding such an alternative school of thought, the odds of the current oqual cycle transitioning into the next one without much noise are however extremely low.

In fact, oqual cycles typically end with a crescendo rather than a whimper.

On the basis of our ongoing dire sociopolitical straits having continued to hit a new low with each passing year since the outset of the 21st century with no signs of reversing the trend, the current oqual cycle indeed appears to be heading for a quasi-apocalyptic end rather than checking out with a relatively mild snowstorm.

Thus, although the doctrine of oqual cycle may suggest that our lives are governed by determinism, it is ultimately our own actions that in fact dictate the severity of the fallout from such a rendezvous with destiny.

While human beings do have the free will to change the course of their rendezvous with destiny so as to eliminate crises and wars (or at least tone them down), their egos almost always get the better of them such that they keep spinning through alternating stages of rebuilding and destruction over what appears to be a period of 84 years.

Long story short, the spell of oqual cycle on human civilization is stochastic (or probabilistic) rather than deterministic in a manner similar to the spell of daily and annual cycles on our lives.

For example, the daily cycle dictates our sleeping and working habits but, ultimately, we can choose not to wake up in the morning or go about our lives.

Likewise, the seasonal changes during the annual cycle provide us with an ample opportunity to make changes to our lives through activities such as planting or harvesting crops but, once again, it is up to us to take advantage of nature's bounties as idle hands reap nothing.

What is the biological significance of oqual cycle?

The oqual cycle lends human society a subtle mechanism to cleanse itself of its wrongdoings (or rectify its errors) lest they snowball into an insoluble labyrinth.

Thus, the oqual cycle essentially serves as a quality control in the progress of human civilization which parallels mechanisms such as backtracking (or proofreading) in cellular polymerases to ensure the fidelity of the product before continuing upstream or further afield.

Ecology also lends a fitting parallel to the importance of oqual cycle.

Just as forest fires eliminate the weed and dead vegetation on the floor so as to clean up and refuel the soil with new nutrients, the oqual cycle is equally necessary to revitalize human society after it reaches its lowest point once in a lifetime, or every 84 years on average.

In analogy with technology, human civilization appears to behave like a desktop computer that begins to slow down after running for some time as it becomes increasingly corrupted due to a myriad of what could be envisaged as unnecessary-and-bureaucratic processes holding its RAM hostage, thereby making it choppy and less productive.

Like a computer, human civilization thus requires a reboot to rid itself of such background noise in order to remain productive and competitive.

Absent an oversight of oqual cycle, humans would be at a disproportional risk of burning themselves out or driving themselves into oblivion due to the buildup of errors in perpetuity and lack of checkpoints in the progress of their civilization.

One cannot imagine life without there being no darkness of the night.

Nor can one imagine life without seasons that shower us with surprises and challenges all year round.

Why one should therefore imagine life without the oqual cycle that seemingly provides an intricately-nuanced mechanism to help us purge our society of all the baggage at periodic intervals, spaced apart by 84 years, so as to ensure that we can continue to plod along with a renewed vigor and energy rather than take the risk of crumbling under its weight.

In a nutshell, the oqual cycle is ultimately a product of evolution in that our biology appears to have gone to great lengths to ensure the long-term survival of its most advanced creation.

Why understanding the oqual cycle is so important?

As the saying goes, those who fail to learn from history are doomed to repeat it.

Admittedly, humans have a notorious reputation for failing to learn from their past mistakes and seemingly indulge in repetitive wrongdoings that plunge our society into a period of extreme trials-and-tribulations once in our lifetime, or once every 84 years on average.

For example, the status quo around the globe marred by dysfunctional and corrupt governments is not only the result of wrong choices made by the-powers-that-be over the past several decades but it has also propelled our society into a sociopolitical upheaval, the like of which we have not witnessed in our lifetime since World War II (1939-1945).

That global conflict all but marked the end of the previous oquannium (1871-1954) and laid the foundations for the beginning of the next cycle (1955-2038) that we are currently navigating.

A corollary of oqual cycle is that, once every 84 years on average, human civilization on the whole:

1) Hits an abyss-of-a-lifetime after its sociopolitical order becomes utterly dysfunctional turning into an insoluble Rubik's cube due to persistent violation of the laws of nature over several decades;

2) Pays the piper or faces a severe retribution in order to redeem and cleanse itself of its malpractices and wrongdoings; and

3) Experiences a sense of rebirth (or renaissance) as it sets about remaking itself in an image that is diametric opposite of its dysfunctional past.

Importantly, such a societal reboot does not occur randomly but rather appears to be more or less synchronized with the orbiting of Uranus around the Sun once every 84 years.

Of particular note is the fact that most nations simultaneously experience a deluge of favorable tailwinds over the course of the first half of oqual cycle followed by a barrage of unfavorable headwinds during the second half in a more or less synchronized manner.

This in-and-of-itself is evidence that the ups and downs in human civilization are not random but rather under the thumb of celestial bodies with Uranus leading the charge.

With an understanding and appreciation of the dire spell of oqual cycle on our lives, not only do we stand to understand ourselves better but the future generations also stand to benefit for they will be handsomely equipped with much knowledge and wisdom so as to minimize the fallout from such calamities that befall humanity once-in-a-lifetime, if not completely bypass them altogether.

|5| GENERATIONS

In sync with the changes in Uranian climate with respect to its southern pole, the oqual cycle is subdivided into a quartet of 21-year seasons chronologically dubbed spring, summer, autumn, and winter.

On average, each one of these four seasons begets a new generational cohort such that one can also view the progression of oqual cycle through the lens of successive generations.

Such a quartet of oqual generations is designated Generation 1 to Generation 4 (G1-G4), which respectively correspond to the four seasons from Spring to Winter.

HOW ONE CAN VIEW THE WAXING AND WANING OF OQUAL CYCLE THROUGH THE LENS OF SUCCESSIVE GENERATIONS

While cascading through a set of four distinct generations (G1-G4), the oqual cycle begins with a honeymoon in spring, undergoes a sense of awakening during summer, begins to unravel with the arrival of autumn, and ends in a cataclysmic crisis in winter in order to cleanse out the old system and herald a new dawn.

Simply put, during times of crisis in the midst of oqual winter particularly circa annus horribilis, people not only gel together to overcome shared agonies and sufferings but also agree to come to a consensus in a non-partisan manner after having navigated to a sociopolitical abyss.

The post-crisis First Generation (G1) born during oqual spring, under the clout of renewed cultural growth and a heightened sense of community coupled with institutional trust, has it much easier because their parents bore the brunt of the woes so that their children would be spared the throes.

As G1 comes of age during oqual summer, the Second Generation (G2) begins to take hold against the backdrop of the society undergoing a period of awakening so as to challenge the authority of elders and the status quo.

Having forgotten to learn the lessons from the trials-and-tribulations that their parents and grandparents had to endure during the preceding oqual winter marred by a crisis of epic proportions, G1 and G2 begin to unravel and break away from the greater good of the society in order to pursue selfish individualism during oqual autumn as the Third Generation (G3) crops up.

The resulting societal entropy (or disorder) ushers in a crisis-of-a lifetime as the final and Fourth Generation (G4) of oqual cycle emerges during a period of sociopolitical bedlam in the midst of oqual winter.

Notably, such a generational model parallels the open secret that the wealth rarely lasts beyond four generations in that the riches of one generation become diluted with each successive generation through the extravaganza and reckless squandering of the wealth by their children and grandchildren such that the great-grandchildren are unlikely to shower in the fruits of the intense labor of their great-grandparents.

Yet, in many ways, the seeds of such wealth destruction were planted in parallel with the accumulation of wealth by the first generation in that its hard work made life easy for their children who in turn made it even easier for their own children such that these subsequent generations not only ended up losing zest for life but also their trove of treasure handed down to them.

Consistent with this notion, one can then also view the waxing and waning of human progress over the course of oqual cycle due to differential challenges placed upon successive generations as follows (see Exhibit 5.1):

1) During oqual winter, hard times carve out a commendable generation of strong people on the back of hard lessons.

2) During the following oqual spring, strong people bring about good times thanks to their selflessness, hard work, and high moral compass.

3) As the oqual summer sets in, good times inevitably beget a despicable generation of weak people with the urge for hedonistic pleasure aplenty but the will for making sacrifices as rare as diamonds—this is due to the lack of challenging times in their lives as a result of the hard work of their parents and grandparents having made life so easy such that it is being taken for granted.

4) Upon the arrival of oqual autumn, weak people begin to dismantle the very values that made their parents and grandparents so successful in life—such unavoidable violation of the basic laws of nature unsurprisingly returns the human society back to square one, or the crisis-of-a-lifetime, during the oqual winter.

Long story short, a rendezvous-with-destiny is therefore not only inevitable but it also seems to be a prerequisite for bringing about a reset (or revolution) in our sociopolitical order so as to break ties with the past and purge the society of a plethora of wrongdoings—from the societal ills through excesses and imbalances to transgressions—amassed over the course of oqual cycle in an attempt to herald a new dawn of hope and prosperity.

OQUAL CYCLE DIFFERENTIALLY SHAPES GENERATIONAL COHORTS

Most of us are familiar with the so-called "cultural generations" such as the Boomers and the Millennials in America as fed to the masses by media pundits and further espoused by the work of Strauss and Howe in their 1991 book titled "Generations" [9].

Not only do such cultural generations vary from one nation to another but they also stretch over a differential timespan of as little as a decade to as much as three decades.

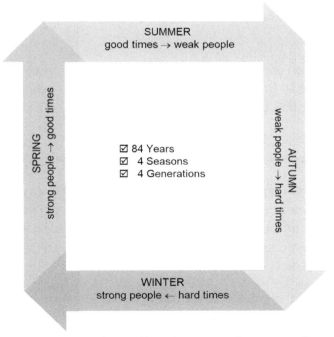

Exhibit 5.1 | Human progress can be envisioned to wax and wane over the course of oqual cycle due to differential challenges placed upon successive generations during each season. In disguise of the novelist Michael Hopf [10], hard times create strong people during oqual winter. Strong people create good times during oqual spring. Good times create weak people during oqual summer. Weak people create hard times during oqual autumn. And the whole cycle repeats itself over a period of 84 years.

To add insult to injury, such groupings of individuals are predicated on the personal viewpoint of none other than the tail that wags the dog.

In marked contrast, the oqual generations are based on a scientific and logical approach in that each generation is:

1) Named First through Fourth in a sequential order;
2) Universal in that it is applicable to every nation across the globe;
3) Fixed in length spanning a period of exactly 21 years;
4) Coincident with an oqual (or Uranian) season; and
5) A recurring archetype that remerges with each spell of oqual cycle.

In a nutshell, not only do oqual generations span a fixed timespan but they also form a constellation with their respective archetypes (or predecessors) from previous oqual cycles.

For example, the First Generation (G1) of every oqual cycle can be grouped (or clustered) together into a unique constellation that shares a similar societal outlook on life, albeit to a varying degree for each one of its archetypes, just as one annual winter is different from another but nevertheless all winters share the same core structure.

Simply put, one can group together oqual generations across all oqual cycles into four constellations (A-D) with each housing one of the four generations (G1-G4)—thus, all G1 generations belong to one unique constellation, ditto for G2 generations, and so forth.

How does the oqual cycle create such generational constellations?

During the course of oqual cycle, progressive sociopolitical forces—such as morality, peace, collectivism, globalism, entrepreneurship, moderation, transparency, nonpartisanship, ethnic harmony, baby boom, economic well-being, and institutional trust—steadily rise over the first half followed by a more-or-less symmetrical drop during the second half.

On the other hand, regressive sociopolitical forces—such as immorality, conflict, individualism, populism, fraud, debt, corruption, partisanship, xenophobia, baby bust, wealth polarization, and institutional distrust—decline over the first half of oqual cycle but rear their ugly head as they begin to precipitously surge during the second half (see Exhibit 5.2).

Such an asymmetrical contribution of various sociopolitical headwinds and tailwinds across the two halves differentially shapes the characteristics or perception of the worldview of various generations that emerge during the course of oqual cycle (see Exhibit 5.3).

For example, individuals born during the winter (G4) of an oqual cycle by-and-large hold a positive view of the society since much of their adult lives coincide with the first half, inundated with plenty of optimism and prosperity, of the next cycle.

Admittedly, most individuals born during the winter (1934-1954) of the previous oquannium (1871-1954) have held the society and institutions in a rather high esteem till quite recently since the sociopolitical system largely worked for the masses throughout much of their adult lives coincident with the first half (1955-1996) of the current oquannium (1955-2038)—and many of such individuals still continue to subscribe to that view even in the face of utter sociopolitical chaos unfolding before their eyes.

In marked contrast, individuals born during the summer (G2) of an oqual cycle by-and-large hold a negative view of the society since much of their adult lives coincide with the second half, mired in utter chaos and sociopolitical upheaval, of the same cycle.

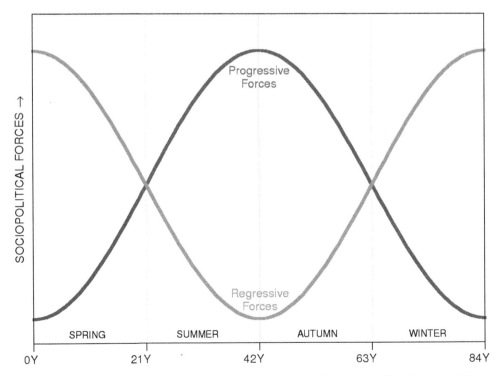

Exhibit 5.2 | The antagonistic roles of progressive and regressive sociopolitical forces in driving the oqual cycle in that they mirror each other across its full span.

Indeed, most individuals born during the summer (1976-1996) of the current oquannium (1955-2038) view the society as largely a collection of oppressive institutions whose goal is to enslave and exploit the masses in that the sociopolitical system has been rigged in favor of a small minority of wealthy and elite throughout what has hitherto been much of their adult lives during the second half (1997-2038).

On the other hand, individuals born during the spring (G1) and the autumn (G3) of an oqual cycle by-and-large hold a rather mixed perception of the society between the two extremes noted above.

Thus, individuals born during the spring (1955-1975) of the current oquannium (1955-2038) generally view the society as so-so since much of their adult lives have straddled across both the first half and the second.

Likewise, individuals born during the autumn (1997-2017) of the current oquannium (1955-2038) are also poised to view the society as so-so since much of their adult lives will be straddling across the second half of the current cycle and the first half of the next one.

Importantly, like the ducklings of the winter (1934-1954) of the previous oquannium (1871-1954), the sucklings born during the winter (2018-2038) of the current oquannium (1955-2038) will also see the world through rose-colored glasses as they come of age.

Oqual Constellation	Oqual Generation	Oqual Season	Societal Outlook	Individuals Born During:		
				OC7	OC6	OC5
A	G1	Spring	Mixed	1955-1975	1871-1891	1787-1807
B	G2	Summer	Negative	1976-1996	1892-1912	1808-1828
C	G3	Autumn	Mixed	1997-2017	1913-1933	1829-1849
D	G4	Winter	Positive	2018-2038	1934-1954	1850-1870

Exhibit 5.3 | Each oqual generation from First through Fourth (G1-G4) across all oqual cycles (though only the three most recent ones are indicated) can be grouped together into one of the four unique constellations color-coded and dubbed A-D. Within each constellation, the recurring generations share a similar societal outlook. For example, the G4 generation born during the winter (2018-2038) of the current and seventh oqual cycle (OC7) will by-and-large hold a positive view of the society in a manner akin to its archetypes born during the winter (1934-1954) of the sixth (OC6) and the winter (1850-1870) of the fifth (OC5) oqual cycles.

In fact, today's infants and toddlers along with the babies born over the next decade or so will be the luckiest-in-a-lifetime as they will come out of their shells into a world full of optimism and prosperity under the clout of renewed cultural growth and a heightened sense of community coupled with institutional trust and a functional government that will once again deliver for the masses.

I should add that those planning to have a baby in the near future must do so by no later than annus mirabilis (2039) of the next oquannium (2039-2122) lest they come of age in a world where a pair of rose-colored glasses once again begins to break their bank as it has been doing so over the past several decades.

Notwithstanding this rationale, the birth rate however typically spikes during the oqual spring rather than oqual winter after all the dust from the fallout of sociopolitical upheaval has settled.

Admittedly, the oqual spring (1955-1975) of the current oquannium (1955-2038) witnessed an unprecedented upsurge in baby boom across the globe with the world population having skyrocketed by almost 50% against the backdrop of relatively prosperous times.

While that scenario is unlikely to pan out during the oqual spring (2039-2059) of the next oquannium (2039-2122) due to the planet already being overpopulated, a baby boom is nevertheless on the cards as the curtain is raised over the next cycle in about a decade or so, thereby putting an end to the rather measly birth rate being witnessed today.

On a personal note, having been born in 1971 on the cusp of spring-summer of the current oquannium (1955-2038), I had been baffled all my life as to why my mentors and seniors born a generation or two before me during the winter (1934-1954) of the previous oquannium (1871-1954) always saw the world through rose-colored glasses when my own experiences were the diametric opposite.

Not only did I begin to lose trust in almost every institution, particularly in the wake of the self-destructive 9/11 Wars waged to merely bloat the pockets of the ruling elite at the expense of killing and uprooting millions, but it even provoked my literary mind to coin catchphrases in order to capture a rising wave of corrupt and fraudulent behavior in our society that I have witnessed over the past quarter-of-a-century as idiomatically expressed below:

> "The doctors have their best interests at your carte (or card) rather than your best interests at their heart!"

> "Beware of lawyers! The only law they practice is how to rip one off and then get away with it in broad daylight!"

"Be mindful of big enchiladas promoting a financial product! The odds of it being a fraud are all but unity!"

"While taking a stroll down the street, one should be more mindful of getting shot by the cops at point-blank range rather than getting mugged!"

Guided by the oqual theory, no longer do I remain baffled about my past experiences nor do I continue to hold the misguided view that perhaps my mentors and seniors were simply naïve and ingenuous but rather our experiences are shaped by the differential spell of oqual cycle on our lives.

It matters a lot not only where we are born but also when we are born.

Though we still remain clueless as to how we are born and why we are born.

Nevertheless, such is the power of oqual cycle as it not only arms one to improve their optics through a circular prism like never before but it also equips them to decode almost every human behavior and societal phenomenon that befalls us.

In short, the oqual theory argues that we are not only connected to our past via our genotype (or DNA) but also through our phenotype (or characteristics) due to the cyclical nature of our civilization.

HOW CAN OQUAL CYCLE HELP ME RATIONALIZE MY OWN SUCCESSES AND FAILURES IN LIFE

The readers should note how successes and failures in their own lives waxed and waned in parallel with the rhythm of oqual cycle.

This is due to the fact that the prevailing sociopolitical atmosphere at each stage of one's life intricately determines their fate.

For example, as a university professor in the field of biomedical research who began to apply his trade at the outset of the 21st century just as the current oquannium (1955-2038) had taken a turn for the worst, I should have been mindful of the dire spell of its ugly second half (1997-2038) that has hitherto spared few in academia.

Tellingly, among a wide array of academic scientists of my generation, I have only once-in-a-blue-moon come across someone who is even barely satisfied with how things have turned out for what they had perceived to be a rather prestigious and fruituous (or fructuous) career choice during their college years against the backdrop of then relatively prosperous and upbeat times—though such happy times were on their last leg as most of us would be left stranded in the middle of nowhere rather than being given a ride off into the sunset.

Little any of us would have known during our good old college years that we would come of age during times of a rising wave of sociopolitical upheaval that would accompany us from our heydays till well into our old age—and that we will never see good times in spite of having sacrificed our lives for a career that we took to heart with all our passion and zest abound.

Rather than being rewarded for our ingenuity and dedication to a career that only the brightest in the society stand a chance of pursuing, the-powers-that-be made us feel like "criminals" and put us through so much "interrogation" that it almost became impossible to do the science that we had dreamed of during our college years.

Indeed, most of us would wholeheartedly attest to the fact that such a bureaucratic red tape made us squander most of our precious time and resources that we ought to have devoted to what we loved most.

To add salt to our proverbial wounds, an overwhelming majority of us would even switch fields to pursue the utter garbage that had become politically "popular" and easily "fundable" rather than what would set our pulse racing every morning.

Necessity may be the mother of invention but the ground-breaking scientific discoveries are the product of pure serendipity—a transition state of nirvana that can only be achieved when scientists are unshackled so as to enable them to pursue the craziest ideas without a bureaucratic oversight for they should not need to justify to anyone why they do what they do for their passion alone is the best metric of their productivity and promise of what they stand to deliver for the society-writ-large.

Admittedly, it is therefore hardly surprising that scientific discoveries by-and-large appear to have hit a roadblock during the second half (1997-2038) of the current oquannium (1955-2038) and arguably pale in comparison to what the generations before us unearthed during the first half (1955-1996)—that was made possible in no small part due to there being relatively prosperous times when bureaucracy took the backseat and allowed scientists to unleash their full potential without becoming entangled in the sociopolitical drama.

That is all the more damning given that the rather paltry bucket-load of dollars allocated toward scientific research during the second half of the 20th century pale in comparison to the humongous ocean-load of funds that have already been squandered during the first quarter of the 21st century alone—thanks to the bureaucratic and wasteful practice of today's corrupt and fraudulent institutions having adopted and normalized a culture of ever-diminishing returns on research dollars.

Against the backdrop of such a pandemonium and powered by their deadly motto of "Fake it till you make it!", the second half (1997-2038) of the current oquannium (1955-2038) has unsurprisingly bred a growing generation of fraudsters and charlatans who have exploited the equally-fraudulent institutional system to steal most of the resources away from bona-fide scientists bereft of projecting such a misleading caricature.

In nature, the opposites attract.

But, it is the "likes" that have attracted the "likes" vis-à-vis the funding of scientific research over the past quarter-of-a-century—a fraudulent institutional system only stands to resonate with fraudsters and their shenanigans.

Even Nobel prizes have become so politicized that they are now being handed out to devious actors a la Gore (2007), Obama (2009), and Bernanke (2022) who have blood on their hands respectively through promoting the climate propaganda so as to divert attention away from pressing issues affecting the well-being of our planet, waging immoral wars to annihilate humanity out of the devilish urge to control and subjugate the weak, and wrecking the financial system so as to ravage the livelihoods of billions around the globe.

These are all signs of the times when nature wages a war of its own to push back against the self-proclaimed Gog and Magog and, in doing so, it purges the society of utter evil so as to give humanity a fresh start.

However, the honeymoon period barely lasts more than a few decades before the likes of Gog and Magog take root once more and bring the society into utter disrepute every 84 years on average as exquisitely embodied in the oqual cycle.

|6| EPILOGUE

Since the outset of the current oquannium (1955-2038), a slew of imbalances and transgressions have once again become endemic to human society at every sociopolitical level.

To right the wrong, humans are therefore set for yet another rendezvous with destiny that arrives on our shores once every 84 years on average.

While such a meeting with destiny cannot be averted, how we deal with the fallout from the ongoing sociopolitical upheaval will determine our fate.

Bluntly put, how one approaches the looming crisis will determine how well one emerges on the other side of the bedlam.

Impulsive actions combined with egoism spell trouble, while thoughtful choices in conjunction with humility stand to assuage the wrath of the emerging crisis.

Thus, although the doctrine of oqual cycle may suggest that our lives are governed by determinism, it is ultimately our free will that in fact dictates the severity of the fallout from such a perennial rendezvous.

For example, no one doubts that our lives are to a large extent governed by the annual cycle.

One can predict with reasonable accuracy that the April showers will bring May flowers in spring, summer will be marred by humidity and hurricanes, crops will be harvested and leaves will fall in autumn, and frigid nights along with snowstorms will be a hallmark of winter.

On the same token, the recurring spell of oqual cycle on human civilization is also punctuated with a quartet of Uranian seasons from spring through summer and autumn to winter—with each season lasting a timespan of 21 years.

In a manner that we can forecast the terrestrial year ahead with some semblance of accuracy, the oqual cycle also equips us with breathtaking insights into what is in store for humanity over the coming decades.

Since the birth of Modern Age in 1451, human civilization has all but spanned seven full spells of oqual cycle.

Today, we are in the early stages of a long and dark 21-year winter (2018-2038) of the seventh oquannium (1955-2038) that is set to reach its crescendo and unleash the worst of its destructive rage upon our civilization as it marks its annus horribilis (2028) with our day of reckoning inching ever closer.

In particular, oqual winters are renowned for staging the collapse of old-and-degenerate sociopolitical orders so as to make way for a brighter dawn.

In 2023, we are more or less passing through the same constellation as we did exactly 84 years ago in 1939 in a manner akin to the fact that annual festivities bring a familiar atmosphere from one year to the next.

In other words, the ongoing oqual winter (2018-2038) is beginning to bear many echoes of the previous oqual winter (1934-1954).

How come have I never heard of the oqual winter?

Unlike the more familiar annual winter that an individual on average traverses dozens of times, the oqual winter comes only once in our lifetime and, even then, very few us have the logic to connect the dots.

For example, an individual born with the onset of the previous oqual winter (1934-1954) was not only too young but also shielded from having to experience the catastrophes that their parents had to endure from the Great Depression (1929-1939) through World War II (1939-1945) to Holocaust (1941-1945).

Today, being in the early stages of the ongoing oqual winter (2018-2038), that now-elderly-individual has virtually no firsthand memories of the previous oqual winter (1934-1954) in order to draw comparisons between the recurrence of two events roughly spaced apart by 84 years.

Still, many elderly people would tell you that they see many parallels between what they witnessed during their early childhood and what is unfolding today before their eyes.

In fact, I have been fortunate enough to personally talk to a number of octogenarians and nonagenarians—individuals who are aged 80-89 and 90-99 years, respectively.

They all confide in me that not only have they never seen anything like what they are experiencing today in their prolonged lives but that they always thought that they had already seen the worst—except of course that their memories of the previous oqual winter (1934-1954) have all but faded.

In order for humans to directly attest to the recurrence of hell-on-earth once every 84 years on average, they will have to live through at least a couple of full spells of oqual cycle disguised as tortoises with a lifespan long enough to meet such stringent criteria.

Alternatively, one could summon an elderly tortoise and they will indeed tell you that nothing could be closer to the truth than the dire spell of oqual cycle that they have to negotiate at least a couple of times in their adult lives.

To add icing on the cake, the anecdotes of tortoises come straight from the horse's mouth for they have no intention of pursuing a political career, much less running for the nation's highest office, or even tweaking climate models to help their cronies make a killing on introducing new consumer products under the guise of environment-friendly technology.

Long story short, what we have seen over the past several years since the onset of the current oqual winter (2018-2038) has hitherto amounted to nothing more than run-of-the-mill snowstorms with the once-in-a-lifetime blizzard yet to unleash its rage upon humanity.

In fact, comparisons between what humanity is going through today with what it did in the aftermath of 1929 Great Depression are far from being in short supply.

Just as that crisis-of-a-lifetime plunged the human society into a global conflict some 84 years earlier, we are once again heading into uncharted waters.

A global conflict is indeed all but obligatory to drive the final nail into the coffin of sociopolitical upheaval, that seemingly snowballs into an 800-pound gorilla as the oqual rhythm nears its end, in order to make way for a new dawn of optimism and prosperity.

Just as World War II (1939-1945) accomplished that goal some 84 years ago so will World War III over the next decade or so as utter fear and chaos engulf our society and, in doing so, purge humanity of mischief so as to enable it to come to its senses once more.

While we have been kicking the can down the road since at least the outset of 21st century, the cul-de-sac (or dead end) is inching ever closer as we are destined to reach there some time between annus horribilis (2028) of the current oquannium (1955-2038) and annus mirabilis (2039) of the next cycle (2039-2122).

All told, the oqual cycle lends a powerful model for not only making sense of the ongoing sociopolitical trials-and-tribulations of our own times but it also helps us navigate our future with rational wisdom in lieu of blissful ignorance.

Those who ignore the spell of oqual cycle will be doing so at their own peril.

In fact, groundbreaking discoveries are always met with skepticism at first and the oqual cycle being disregarded by the trawler and its entourage of seagulls is inevitable until it becomes widely accepted with the passage of time in a stunning echo of humanity's perpetual failure to pay heed to dire lessons of history.

For example, the notion that the Earth orbits the Sun was first proposed by Copernicus in 1515 but this so-called heliocentric view of our world would draw the ire of the clergy and continued to be mocked by fools and horses over the course of the next couple of centuries during which many who dared to subscribe to such a doctrine were either vilified or charred to death.

Even the likes of Galileo, Kepler, and Newton would be reprimanded for subscribing to what was then believed to be a heretic view at odds with religion during much of the 16th and 17th centuries, and it was not until 1758 that the church finally dropped its opposition to heliocentrism and only then it would go mainstream.

Just as the heliocentric model of our world stood the test of time so will the theory of oqual cycle though none of us alive today will unfortunately be around to celebrate its homecoming-in-earnest.

In closing, the oqual cycle forecasts the following prophecies to come to fruition some time during the decade beginning with annus horribilis (2028) of the current oquannium (1955-2038) and ending with annus mirabilis (2039) of the next cycle (2039-2122) so as to herald the true spirit of a global reset:

1) **Stock Market**—Having been inflated by cheap money for more than a decade, the stock-market bubble will pop and wipe off the life-savings of decamillions in America in an echo of the 1929 crash and making the 2008 financial meltdown look like a dress rehearsal. This is necessary to purge the gunk and fraud out of the financial system that has been gathering momentum over the past several decades in order to lend humanity a fresh start on its economic front with the arrival of a new oqual cycle. The European markets will likely fare much better given that money printing had little impact on their valuations as they have largely continued to remain depressed rather than having bloated a la their counterparts on the other side of the Atlantic.

2) **Real Estate**—Having been inflated by cheap money for more than a decade, the real-estate bubble across much of the globe will come down crashing so as to bring the property values in line with the earning power of an average household. In particular, the rather bloated valuation of commercial properties will bear the brunt of the wrath of oqual cycle as it draws to a close. In the wake of the 2019 Coronavirus Pandemic, the tectonic shift to conducting personal and business affairs online in lieu of office will also eat into the demand for commercial real estate, thereby further exacerbating the pain for real-estate moguls.

3) **Bank Failures**—Due to being overleveraged with mountains of debt coupled with their fraudulent practices, thousands of zombie companies will go belly up and, in doing so, they will also put thousands of their stakeholders such as lenders and banks underwater. The mainstream propaganda continues to indoctrinate the masses that the banks are well-capitalized and that the

financial system is sound and resilient. Nothing could be further from the truth. In fact, the very argument that the banks are well-capitalized is an oxymoron in that money loaned out to businesses and consumers at any given time is multiples greater than a bank's actual worth of deposits courtesy of the so-called fractional-reserve banking. During good times, such exorbitant lending is not an issue as a booming economy pays for itself. However, during hard times as is the case across much of the globe today, most borrowers are overleveraged to the hilt, not to mention that many startups that have borrowed billions from banks only exist on paper with nothing to show for except bogus products that will never see the light of day. Once such fraudulent companies go up in smoke as they are poised to do so over the next decade due to the dire spell of oqual cycle as it nears its end, they will take what are being portrayed as sound-and-resilient banking institutions down with them too. With a number of banks having already gone belly up this year, the bank failures are not only just getting started but they will also make the fall of banking dominoes one after another during the Great Depression (1929-1939) look like a child's play. Notably, it was not the subprime mortgage per se that precipitated the 2008 Financial Crisis but rather the big banks were brought down to their knees due to being overleveraged through uber-risky and ultra-speculative derivative trading. Today, such derivative trading on the part of big banks is multiples greater and, as such, their looming failures will likely dwarf what transpired some 15 years ago. In the context of the dire spell of oqual cycle, the 2008 Financial Crisis was a dress rehearsal for what is lurking on the horizon as we inch ever closer to our day of reckoning.

4) **Social Security**—Failed socialist experiments such as America's Social Security Administration (1935) and UK National Assistance Act (1948) that vowed to take care of people from the cradle to the grave beginning almost in parallel with the arrival of the current oquannium (1955-2038) will practically become defunct and worthless in that they will be inflated away and the handouts furnished to recipients will barely pay for peanuts, much less everyday cost of living. With the welfare paychecks being handed out to people across much of the Western world having already significantly fallen behind the cost of living due to soaring inflation over the past decade or so, one can already smell the beginning of the end of social security as we have known it in our lifetime.

5) **Reserve Currency**—The USD will lose its monopoly of being the global reserve currency and make way for CNY (or CNY-in-disguise of another currency) to emerge as the new dominant player in international trade. This is hardly a brainer given that the major global currency almost always belongs to the

nation that has proven itself as the manufacturing powerhouse head-and-shoulders above its competitors as the oqual cycle draws to a close. Nevertheless, USD will remain a major player in international trade though in the shadow of CNY in a manner akin to what happened to GBP after it was dethroned by the dollar thanks to the 1944 Bretton-Woods Agreement. With the dollar no longer being the king, the standard of living in America will precipitously decline in an echo of the plight of the British after the pound lost its global luster some 84 years ago.

6) **Chinese Hegemony**—China will undergo reunification with Taiwan as it knocks America off the perch to become the new hegemon and tiktoks the new world order centered around its national interests. As China's star rises and that of America dims with each passing year, it is hard to see how such a reunification central to Chinese hegemony can be averted, particularly in light of the fact that the territorial disputes are at the center of the mayhem trigged by the oqual cycle as it reaches its crescendo. Nevertheless, United States will continue to be a major global power in a manner akin to the fact that the British influence on global affairs did not merely evaporate from the planet after Britain was dethroned some 84 years ago. Just as the legacy of the British Empire left an indelible mark on human civilization so will American imprint continue to thrive for at least generations to come across the globe.

7) **Global Warming**—The climate propaganda will largely die out as environmental focus will shift from global warming to dealing with the true culprit of overconsumption putting the health of our planet in peril. Given that the root cause of our environment teetering on the precipice of a mental collapse is the pollution caused by overconsumption rather than fossil fuels, truth rather than propaganda will ultimately prevail with the beginning of a new dawn. The rather auspicious spell of the first half (2039-2080) of the next oquannium (2039-2122) will also ensure that societal evils such as fraud and propaganda are locked up for the most part for at least several decades though they will slowly begin to re-emerge from the silos with the onset of the second half (2081-2122).

|7| LITERATURE

1. Modelski G (1987). Long Cycles in World Politics. Palgrave Macmillan (London, England, UK).

2. Strauss W and Howe N (1997). The Fourth Turning: An American prophecy. Broadway Books (New York, New York, USA).

3. Turchin P (2016). Ages of Discord: A Structural-Demographic Analysis of American History. Beresta Books (Chaplin, Connecticut, USA).

4. Spengler O (1918). The Decline of the West. Allen & Unwin (London, England, UK).

5. Toynbee AJ (1934). A Study of History: Volumes I-XII (1934-1961). Oxford University Press (Oxford, England, UK).

6. National Aeronautics and Space Administration (2023). Space Missions: Voyager 2. https://solarsystem.nasa.gov/missions/voyager-2/in-depth.

7. Kent DV, Olsen PE, Rasmussen C, Lepre C, Mundil R, Irmis RB, Gehrels GE, Giesler D, Geissman JW, and Parker WG (2018). Empirical evidence for stability of the 405-kiloyear Jupiter-Venus eccentricity cycle over hundreds of millions of years. Proceedings of the National Academy of Sciences of the United States of America **115**, 6153-6158.

8. Killion N (2008). Life Cycles. AuthorHouse (Bloomington, Indiana, USA).

9. Strauss W and Howe N (1991). Generations: The History of America's Future. William Morrow and Company (New York, New York, USA).

10. Hopf GM (2014). The End: A Postapocalyptic Novel. Plume (New York, New York, USA).

The author is Associate Professor in the Department of Biochemistry at the University of Miami Miller School of Medicine in South Florida.

Although a biophysicist by trade with close to 100 scientific publications, Professor Farooq is best characterized as a polymath whose working knowledge transcends fields as diverse as astronomy, economy, climatology, psychology, sociology, geopolitics, linguistics, history, and religion.

Amjad Farooq

Powered by such polymathy coupled with a fearless mind renowned for pulling no punches, this book presents what is nothing short of being a Rosetta stone of human civilization to add to a breath of fresh air and candor rarely on display in today's society mired in sociopolitical upheaval.

A once-in-a-millennium book and straight from the horse's mouth, The Oqual Cycle brings about a paradigm shift in how we view the world and our own place within it and, as such, it is a must-read for everyone irrespective of their national, ethnic, political, and religious affiliation.

Human civilization waxes and wanes over a period of 84 years

OQUANNIUM
XPRESS

Printed in Great Britain
by Amazon

26425716R00057